'Who Touched Me?'

Gillian Edgar

New Wine Press

New Wine Press
PO Box 17
Chichester
England PO20 6YB

ISBN 1 903725 27 5

Typeset by CRB Associates, Reepham, Norfolk.
Printed in England by Clays Ltd, St Ives plc.

Dedication

I would like to take this opportunity to thank all those people who cared for and nursed me through the many difficult years of my illness.

I would also like to thank my many friends for their advice, support and encouragement in getting this book published.

I dedicate *Who Touched Me?* to my two sons, Matthew and Daniel. Thank you both for your cheerfulness, courage and unconditional love.

'If only I may touch His garment
I shall be made well'
(Matthew 9:21)

Contents

Foreword

Putting pen to paper in order to write this book has not been easy. Some of the things shared I would have preferred to keep secret. However, being totally honest and open to God is how He likes us to be. Nothing is hidden from His sight. So, in my 'openness', I hope you will see how God can forgive the most hopeless sinner, heal the pain of mistakes, guilt and regrets and give the opportunity for a fresh start in life.

The miracle of salvation remains the most important of gifts.
My miracle of healing was a bonus.

I do not wish to offend anyone by this book and so some of the names of the people have been changed to protect their privacy.

Re: Mrs Gillian Edgar

Thank you for allowing me to see Mrs Edgar. She has not been at all well, and required a home visit, which I did at the above address on the 24 January 1988.

This lady started an illness in 1984 from which she has not recovered. She describes waking up in the middle of the night with palpitation, pins and needles, pains in her wrists, knees and ankles, and profuse sweating, feeling ill and tired, rather like getting 'flu.

She visited her Doctor a few days later, and was told that she probably had a panic attack, and clearly there were a number of reasons for suggesting that possible diagnosis, in that she has had a great deal of stress and strain in the previous years. But for the next couple of years, after recovering from this initial episode, she never quite returned to her old self. She continued to work as a nursery teacher, but part-time, as the result of a head injury a year previously, but found that she was not getting her words out correctly. They would come out back-to-front, and often incorrect, not infrequently making her subjects and children laugh at her.

She began getting rather forgetful and she noticed also that everything she did was an effort, making her feel fatigued and unwell. She noticed that all of these symptoms would be made worse if she went for a walk or if she had a lot of hassle and anxiety, stress or strain. This would then put her in bed for the next day, after which she would recover from the sudden exacerbation in her bodily fatigue.

The situation remained about the same for the next couple of years. Then, for no obvious reason but probably as the result of working too hard, the symptoms got worse. By June 1987 after an attack of food poisoning, her condition worsened and she has never fully recovered, and she has not been back to work.

On a good day she is just about able to get out of bed and manage to muddle about the house. On a bad day she spends most of her time in bed. Her bad days consist of two or three days per week. She notes that all of her symptoms are made worse by exercise of any degree, and only alleviated by resting. Her symptoms are very variable and include an indescribable feeling of being ill, and total exhaustion. She has great difficulty getting out of bed to go to the loo, complains of muscle twitching, shortness of breath and palpitations, insomnia, nightmares, loss of concentration and memory, sore glands in her neck axilla and groin, feeling hot and cold, and being a ghastly grey pallor when she is ill.

In her previous history, from a physical point of view, she was diagnosed as having Crohn's disease some twenty years ago. She receives no medication and has had a chronic bowel problem ever since. She had a fibroid adenoma removed from her right breast, a severe head injury a year previously to this particular episode, after which she suffered head-aches, tinitus and giddiness, but none of the physical symptoms that she describes in her body now.

She has had a lot of trauma over the last few years, including a break up of her marriage, death of a close aunt and her house burning down. However, she feels that her symptoms, whatever they are, are purely physically based, and are not either hysterical, conversional or depressive.

From my point of view, I would have thought the story, the symptomatology and clinical fluctuation are typical of Post Viral Syndrome (otherwise known as Myalgic Encephalo-myelitis) and I would suggest that is almost certainly what she has.

In the meantime, as there is no treatment or cure for this disease, and she has made no clinical progress, I would have thought that her chances of making a significant recovery very small.

(Excerpt taken from a medical letter)

PART ONE

Chapter 1

A New Beginning

'Behold, I make all things new.'
(Revelation 21:5)

I awoke as usual, glad that the night was finally over and that a new day had dawned. It had been yet another long and restless night with little sleep, and moments when I felt so desperately ill. Coping alone with a serious illness always seemed more difficult at night. How often I longed for someone to be there who I could turn to for comfort, a reassuring word or a gentle touch. I looked upon each night with fear and dread of the unknown, and so I was always relieved to see the dawn and the beginnings of a new day.

It was 7.30 a.m. and I could hear the activities of Matthew and Daniel as they prepared for their day ahead. It had been a long time since I had been able to care for myself, let alone support them, and so our roles had been reversed. We had a good routine worked out; in fact my bedroom had become my survival quarters with mini cooker, kettle, TV and telephone. It was their job to bring everything I might need during the day ahead, before they left for school.

The door opened and in they came bringing trays laden with fruit, milk, china, cutlery, pepper, salt, saucepans, fresh water and tins of soup.

'Morning Mum, glad you're okay, see you later, we've got to dash,' and with a hug, they went off to school. This had been our daily routine for over two-and-a-half years.

I looked around my room. Chaos seemed to be the order of the day, in fact it seemed to be the order of my life. Because of the nature of my illness, I was unable to physically look after myself. Even the simplest of tasks took much effort. Questions would start to flood my mind, would I be able to brush my hair? Clean my teeth? Would I be able to lift the glass of water? Or be able to pull myself out of bed to go to the bathroom? I knew that some days I would not have the energy to speak and would have to have the curtains drawn because the light hurt my eyes.

But this day was going to be different. I was not sure whether I felt excited, afraid, annoyed or embarrassed. I suppose on reflection I felt all of these emotions. I was going to have some visitors. This in itself was something I dreaded and tried to avoid. Talking and having to concentrate always left me drained and would often take me many days to recuperate. I was not really sure how these ladies could help me, but as I realised that I had nothing to lose by their visit, I had agreed to see them.

I pulled myself up against the pillows and caught a glimpse of myself in the mirror. I hardly recognised the face that peered back. I looked gaunt, thin and old. The long period of disability had wasted my muscles and my flesh now hung from my bones. I can tell you I was not a pretty sight! A moment of panic set in. The two women who were coming would probably be smartly dressed. My illness had certainly stripped me of any human pride. Linda and Claire would be arriving at 10.30 a.m. allowing me a little time to try and prepare for their visit. It was a Monday morning, and every Monday, Rachel would come and clean the house and try to tidy up for the boys. Not an easy task, but one that she did with great compassion and care.

She was a real help to me during this time, always sensitive to my needs and willing to do all she could to help.

'Rachel,' I said as she appeared at my door, 'I'm expecting

some friends this morning, and you'll never guess why they are coming to see me.'

She looked puzzled. 'No I can't imagine,' she said.

'They are coming to pray for me,' I answered.

Two days previously, I had a telephone call from a friend whom I had not seen for many years. She had heard of my illness and asked me if she could come and see me and pray for me. I must admit that I found it very hard to agree initially to her request. It was not that I did not believe, in fact I would say that I had a strong faith, but the thought of someone coming specifically to pray out loud, seemed rather intrusive and embarrassing. It was something that was alien to me.

A 10.30 a.m. Claire and Linda arrived. Rachel brought them into my room and then went to make some coffee.

'Whatever must they think of me?' was my first reaction.

I had not been able to wash my hair for days, and how I longed for a real bath (taking a bath would leave me totally exhausted for days and so were few and far between). However, they seemed to be oblivious to my thoughts, and taking off their coats, sat down and smiled at me.

They immediately started to talk about their faith and their personal relationship with Jesus Christ. It was obvious to me that Jesus was as tangible to them, as they were to me at that moment in my room. It was an amazing revelation to hear them talk about Him in that way. I had never met anyone before who had had their experience. It was as if Jesus Himself was visiting me, and I knew that I too wanted to know Him in the same way. Their faces radiated happiness and their peace was something deep within them. It was something I lacked in my faith but could recognise now the reality and truth of their Christian lives, and I too wanted to have what they had.

'Have you given your life to the Lord?' they asked.

I felt as if an arrow had pierced my own heart as I began to think about my own Christian life and upbringing. I had always considered myself to be a Christian, although I must admit I was aware of a huge gap between God in heaven and me down here, but I presumed like most people that death would inevitably lead to heaven.

My mother had brought me up in the Church of England doctrine. I was baptised as a baby and confirmed as a young teenager. In fact I had vivid memories of my Confirmation service, not for what was said by any Bishop, but for something my mother had told me. I was confirmed with my school friends and my mother had made me a very plain long-sleeved white dress. A few days before the confirmation service a dress rehearsal was held in the church. I put on my dress and then to my horror saw my friends appearing in dresses made of white lace and satin, adorned with bows, buttons and frills. I felt like orphan Annie. I rushed home thinking I could persuade my mother to add a few finishing touches to my dress; after all, I did not want to stand out or be different from the others. The answer I received from her was not the one I had expected or hoped for. She told me that I needed to be plainly and simply dressed when I came before the Lord. That remark made quite an impression upon my young mind.

I then began to think back to another experience that I had had when I was about seven years old. I remember making up a nursery rhyme as I jumped up and down on my bed. It went something like this:

'One, two, three, four, five, six, seven
Shut those gates that lead to heaven.'

I can recall the feeling of horror as the words left my mouth. It filled me with dread that God may have heard me and taken me at my word! I was really upset for weeks.

Linda put down her cup of coffee.

'You have to be saved,' she said. 'You have to be born again. Being a Christian is not something we inherit from our parents' upbringing. Being baptised or confirmed will not save you. It is all about repentance and giving your life to the Lord.'

It began to make sense to me, and looking back over the years, I realised how I had ignored God and how much I must have grieved Him. The burden of my sinful life was all too real for me. If God could do something about that, I did not want to miss the opportunity of making myself right with Him.

'You have to be saved. It is written in God's Word that you must be saved and born again,' said Claire.

I knew that I had to make a decision. I made up my mind to accept Jesus as my Lord and Saviour. I had no idea that what was about to happen to me would change my life totally. The three of us bowed our heads in prayer and I repeated the words Linda prayed.

'Dear Lord, I realise that I am a sinner and I ask You to forgive me. I truly repent and I give You my life. Please come into my life so that I may know You as my Saviour, and baptise me with Your Holy Spirit. Thank You for all You did for me on the cross, for dying for me that I might have eternal life.'

As I was saying my prayer the most amazing things began to happen to me. I could feel a heat come through my body and spread from the top of my head down to my feet. I was burning and yet felt quite comfortable. As I began to thank the Lord for what He had done for me, I began to speak in another language. I could not understand what I was saying. I suppose I felt a little apprehensive and yet calm at the same time. These beautiful words kept flowing from my mouth. I could not have stopped speaking even if I had wanted too. It was wonderful!

Linda and Claire did not seem surprised, but continued praying in tongues, as it is called. I was having the same experience as the first disciples had at Pentecost as they gathered in Jerusalem.

> *'Now when the day of Pentecost had fully come, they were all with one accord in one place. And suddenly there came a sound from heaven, as of a rushing mighty wind, and it filled the whole house where they were sitting. Then there appeared to them divided tongues, as of fire, and one sat upon each of them. And they were all filled with the Holy Spirit and began to speak with other tongues, as the Spirit gave them utterance.'*
> (Acts 2:1–4)

I had received the baptism of the Holy Spirit!

From that moment, I knew I was saved and born again. The date was 7th November 1988. Jesus came into my room and into my life and I had an overwhelming love for Him. The guilt of my sinful life had been lifted from me and I felt as if I had been set free. It was a dramatic conversion and a powerful affirmation that from that moment onwards God would have His hand upon my life. Only He knew what lay ahead for me and of how much I would need to draw from His strength.

Linda and Claire stayed a little longer and we all rejoiced together at what God had done. They had been with me for over two-and-a-half hours! Rachel had left sometime earlier leaving me alone until the boys returned home at 4.30 p.m. The boys! What on earth was I going to say to them and how would I explain the morning's events to my mother? I felt excited for I knew in my heart that there was no need to worry about anything, Jesus was firmly by my side and whatever I may have to go through I would never feel alone again.

Chapter 2

My Childhood Years

'Before I formed you in the womb I knew you . . . '
(Jeremiah 1:5)

I was born on a farm in Worcestershire in the summer of 1943 and remained there during my early childhood. My elder brother David and I were great companions and spent many happy hours growing up in these idyllic settings. I have always been very much aware of the beauty of nature and appreciated the country life. Both my parents shared a great love for horses and subsequently David and I were encouraged to ride from an early age. Sadly, when I was four years old the farm was sold and our peaceful life came to an abrupt end. My mother, who was pregnant, took David and myself to live with her family, while my father returned to stay with his mother. I was to learn in later life that this was the beginning of many hardships my mother had to endure during her years of a very difficult marriage.

My mother was petite in stature, barely reaching five feet tall, but was strong and amazingly tough, often dogmatic, a disciplinarian, outspoken, courageous and brave. She was the most important person in my life. She was my best friend and there was nothing I could not share with her. I loved her with a great passion, although our relationship was not always easy.

My sister, Jennifer, was born while we were living at the home of my grandparents. I can remember clearly the first

Childhood days!

time that David and I were allowed to see her. We both had had an attack of the measles and had to have handkerchiefs tied around our faces before entering the room, where she lay in the 'Moses' basket. We peered into the crib and saw a tiny bundle tightly wrapped in a shawl. We were not able to touch her of course, but I remember being fascinated by this newest member of the family and secretly hoped it would not be too long before I would be able to play with her.

My grandmother was Welsh and had a great influence on the running of the household. I am not sure whether she liked me, but I was very fond of her. My grandfather was bedridden and so any real relationship we may have had was restricted and I rarely visited him in his room. Because of his failing health, we were always conscious that playtimes had to be carried out with the minimum of noise, which was a great hardship to two boisterous children.

Meal times were shared around a large table. Granny would sit at the head of the table with my mother, her elder sister, Enid, and her elder brother, Jack. Meal times were strict and we were expected to eat everything that was placed in front of us. One day we had tapioca for pudding. I looked in horror at my plate of 'frog spawn' and made up my mind that there was no way I was going to let this pudding reach my lips! Who on earth in their right mind would want a stomach full of frogs? I had to sit at the table staring at my plate all afternoon. Eventually, my distraught mother persuaded me to eat a spoonful, and then I was allowed to leave the table.

(P.S. no frogs.)

About eighteen months later, my father, who was a huntsman, accepted employment in Lincolnshire and so we moved from Worcestershire to begin life again as a family. Gone were the big houses and open spaces and we had to quickly adapt to living in a flat above a stable block. It seemed very dark and dreary and to make matters worse, it was next to a derelict ruin that had been gutted by fire. I remember lying awake at night listening to the horses below and being rather frightened by them.

As I continued to grow up, I became increasingly aware of the tremendous love and skill my mother had with horses. There never seemed to be a spare moment when she was not riding. Some of the horses she rode were unpredictable and often extremely dangerous. One day, as she was returning home after a day's hacking, a lorry sped past her, frightening her horse. She was thrown onto the road, and the lorry drove over her. Miraculously, she was only bruised and badly shaken, but it was a terrifying ordeal for me as a six-year-old child to witness. As far as I was concerned, horses were a threat and took my mother away when I needed her. I was never able to share or appreciate this part of my mother's life. Circumstances were different for my sister, and as she grew up, she too became very involved with the horse world.

Life was just beginning to settle for us, when once again we had to move. Out came the packing cases and everything was carefully put away. We would be moving from Lincolnshire to Hampshire to live in the Meon valley. It was a welcome relief to live once again in the heart of the country. My mother quickly made our new house into a home and I have some happy memories of the short time we spent there. Twelve months later, we moved to the 'kennels' on the outskirts of a small village called Droxford. However, after a relatively short time we moved again, this time into the village.

Our schooling had suffered considerably from the constant moves, and so a decision was made that with the financial support of our grandmother, uncle and aunt, we would all be sent to private schools. I was sent to a convent in the nearest town of Wycombe.

The nuns and their way of life fascinated me, but sadly I have to admit that I was made to feel like a 'second class' citizen. Non-Catholics were not allowed to participate in any of the church activities, so we spent considerable time doing 'extra' homework, which I thought was most unfair! I would sit in the classroom, as the sweet aroma of incense filled the school. As mass was celebrated, I would try and imagine what was going on behind the closed doors. The nuns were very strict and we had to keep long periods of silence. One day, I was hit very hard with a ruler across the palm of my hand. I had no idea what I had done to deserve such punishment, but I secretly wondered whether it was because I was not a Catholic. These nuns were no advertisement for the Christian faith, although I am sure there are nuns who know the Lord. However, in spite of having to bow my head and curtsy every time I passed a nun I felt a strange attraction to them. By this time, my mother was beginning to realise that the convent life was not for me, and so I was taken away and sent with Jennifer to a small private school in Fareham.

It was at this time in my life, that I fell in love with the world of ballet, and so my dancing career began like most young girls with lessons on a Saturday afternoon. I was fortunate enough to continue with this serious hobby until well after I had had my children.

As I matured, I became increasingly more self-conscious and insecure. I had worn glasses from the age of two and was often called 'four-eyes' as a joke. This did nothing to promote any self-image that I might have had.

Jennifer was growing up fast and she and David formed a close relationship, and the saying of 'two's company, three's a crowd' became a reality for me and I felt very much alone.

Sundays were always kept special in our home. Mother would always cook a Sunday roast, which we would eat around a large dinning room table, although I can never remember a time when my father joined us. In the evening, she would take us to the church in the village square.

Eventually, the inevitable happened, and mother announced that we would be parting from my father and moving to Worcester. I was not quite sure how I felt about this prospect, but certainly the thought of living near my mother's family was appealing. I had no emotion for my father, except to feel rather sorry for him. What I did not realise, was that I had to stay with a school friend and her family, while my mother left with Jennifer in order to make the necessary arrangements for our future education. David was to be a boarder at the school he was already attending. What I was about to experience was to be one of the most traumatic times of my life. I was so homesick and cried everyday at school and wept every night into my pillow.

Eventually, my mother came back to Hampshire and took me home to Worcester. Six months later, Aunt Enid bought mother a cottage which was to be our first real home, and the one in which my mother lived for the rest of her life.

Chapter 3

Valley of Heartache

'I cry out with my whole heart;
Hear me, O LORD!'
(Psalm 119:145)

If I had felt insecure and shy during my childhood, it was nothing compared with my teenage years. I was fairly happy at my school although I was not very academic. Eventually, I grew up to find myself living in the 'swinging sixties'. I decided the glasses had to go. I put them in a drawer and let my blonde hair grow long. It had the desired effect, but whether I could cope with this sudden attention was a different matter! Going to an 'all girls' school had certainly protected me from the world of boys! Exciting opportunities were there for the taking and I wanted to taste everything and have fun. Many doors were opened for me and I had some wonderful times, but I also regret many of the fruitless things I pursued.

When I was in my late teens, my grandmother had a major heart attack. All the family were called to her bedside to be with her when she died. This was my first experience of looking death in the face, and it had a profound effect upon me. I was naturally very upset, but I was left with this absolute certainty that there must be life after death.

In 1966, when I was in my early twenties I met Peter a divorcee with two small children. A friendship developed between us, and although the responsibility of a long-term commitment did not flourish, I believe that our feelings for each other were genuine.

A year later, in 1967, I met John and we married six months later. We lived together in a flat in Worcester, moving a few months later to another flat in Droitwich. In many ways our marriage started out as fun, based on a mutual friendship, a liking for one another and the ability to discuss anything, although we did not necessarily always agree! We had only been married for six months, when, while on holiday in Spain, I became very ill. On returning to this country, I was admitted onto an isolation ward at Hackney hospital in London, as a suspect case of typhoid. A laparotomy operation was performed and nearly two litres of poison was drained from my stomach. The surgeon later told John that had the operation been delayed a further two hours it would have been too late to save me. Although it was difficult to prove medically, the diagnosis was that I was suffering from Crohn's disease. It took me many months to recover, and subsequently I was kept under observation for a further ten years.

My father, whom I had rarely seen since my childhood, developed cancer. I went to visit him with my uncle John, who was my father's brother. It was an odd meeting as neither my uncle nor myself were close to him. When he died several months later, I cried with regret for the lack of relationship between us. My one consolation was that I got on well with my uncle John and he became my close friend.

Like most married couples, we had our financial burdens, which made it impossible for us even to think about owning a house of our own. My mother's cottage had a large garden and we were given some of this land as a belated wedding present. We managed to obtain planning permission and secured a mortgage.

We designed our very own house that had many unique features and did much of the hard graft ourselves. This project was not without its challenges, but two years later when it was finally completed, we moved back to live in the countryside.

We both wanted a family, but it was not easy for me to become pregnant. I had to undergo many tests and examinations but finally, our sons were born in 1971 and 1974. This time was to be my happiest but sadly, when the boys were still quite young, our marriage started to run into difficulties. My husband had been adopted as a baby and I think this played a big part in his insecurity. I always seemed to have to prove my love for him. He was at times extremely possessive and I began to feel claustrophobic and unfulfilled. I wondered too what was wrong with me and began to question the restlessness I felt within. I knew that in spite of everything, John loved me, I had a beautiful home and two healthy sons, yet surely there must be more to life than this? I felt I was unable to be the person John wanted me to be, and so contention grew between us and our once happy marriage began to crumble.

About this time Aunty Enid also developed cancer and had to have major surgery. She faced her battle with courage but sadly she died quite suddenly just before Christmas Eve 1979. This was a bitter blow as I had always been closely involved with her.

After eight years of marriage, I met Peter again. He had never re-married and we discovered that our feelings for one another had not changed. It was not long before I found that I was in the most appalling situation and completely unable to control my actions, other than to be governed by how I felt. I told John about our friendship because I still had a deep regard for him, and I thought my being honest was the best way of dealing with the situation. Twice I tried to end the relationship with Peter, but I always went back to him.

In the summer of 1981, I discovered that I was pregnant and Peter was the father of my child. John realised that it was now no good hanging on to a sham marriage, and so we parted.

I was devastated. I was in love with Peter, and yet I knew I still cared deeply for John. I also loved the baby I was now carrying. What a mess!

John left and went to stay with his parents who had recently moved to live near us. I was very sad that I had caused them so much pain by the break up of our marriage.

I decided that I would carry on living at our home. I felt alone, but determined that I would find a solution and that everything would be all right. Matthew and Daniel were ten and eight years old respectively. I tried to plan out in my mind what I should do. Both boys were attending a private school and in order to finance their education, I was working as a teacher at a nursery school. I knew that now I would have to give up work, which meant that not only would the boys have to cope without a father, but also have to change schools where they were settled and happy. They would have to get used to a new stepfather and cope with the arrival of a baby all within a few months. I had moments of sheer joy at the prospect of being a mother again, and then moments of utter panic at how hopeless the situation appeared. The only advice my doctor gave me was to have an abortion.

It was at this time that I first cried out to God to help me. I remember sitting on the edge of my bed, sobbing and shaking uncontrollably.

'Oh God! If You are real, reveal Yourself to me,' I cried.

A few moments later, I felt such a peace in my room, and my weeping suddenly stopped. I knew that something supernatural had happened to me. There could be no other explanation. God must have heard me. I arose from my bed and calmly walked down the stairs. I have since often wondered why I walked out of my room so soon. Perhaps if I had stayed and talked to God and sought Him more, I would have been spared many of the heartaches that lay in front of me. Maybe I was a little frightened of the truth, that God had actually heard me, and I did not know how to deal with the implications of what that meant.

Over the next few weeks I agonised as to what I should do. It is true that often you do not realise what you have lost until it is too late. Wounding John in the way I had, now wounded me. Whatever our problems had been, he did not deserve what must have seemed to him as the ultimate betrayal. Yet, even now he still offered his hand to me, but understandably on condition I had an abortion. Peter was supportive but silent, leaving the decision with me. I would lie awake at night talking to my baby, telling him every-thing would be all right. I loved being pregnant again, but in the morning I would be racked with feelings of guilt and shame.

My doctor had given me a telephone number of a clinic where I could have an abortion. I rang and arranged for an interview. I travelled to Birmingham where I was assessed. I was accepted without any question. I was surprised how easy it was. Yet even now I knew in my heart that I did not want to go through with this termination. I waited another two weeks. Another moment of panic sent me back to the tele-phone. I was horrified to find out that I would have to go once again to be assessed, and so I returned to Birmingham.

On the 5th October 1981, I went to have an abortion. I was ten weeks pregnant. I have tried to think exactly how I can put into words my feelings, but I cannot, except to say that it was the most harrowing experience. The baby I loved and wanted, I allowed to be taken from me. I know that ultimately the decision was mine, but such was the burden, that I felt my freedom of choice had to be sacrificed as well. On arrival at the private clinic, I was shown to my room and told to put on a white gown and to wait until I was called. I shared the room with a lovely Irish girl. She was a Catholic, and having brought shame upon her family, had had her abortion arranged by her brother. She had travelled on her own by ferry, and would be returning the next day. I often think of her and wonder what happened to her.

The door was opened and a nurse told us that we would be the next to go to theatre. I said I was not ready and asked if I could see the surgeon, who would be operating on me. I kept thinking, 'If only I did not have to go through with this perhaps the doctor would say it was too late to do it and I would be told to go home . . . '

An Indian doctor appeared and examined me. He said a few words, but reassured me that there was nothing to worry about. After he had gone, I decided to try and ring Peter. He had brought me to the clinic and was staying at a hotel near by. I would ask him to come and fetch me and take me home. I went to the telephone, dialled the number, but there was no reply. My heart sank. Peter told me later that he had gone to sit in a nearby church and that must have been where he was when I tried to contact him. As I walked back to my room, I suddenly thought about asking to see a counsellor. Why had I not thought of that before! She would understand how I felt. I began to get excited.

A few minutes later, a woman appeared and came and sat down on my bed. I poured out my heart to her, but instead of helping me she told me to pull myself together. She told me that the foetus was only a blob of cells. Any glimmer of hope now left me, as she took me by the hand and led me to the theatre. I have often seen pictures of the Jews being led to the concentration camps and ultimately the gas chambers, and for a few moments I thought perhaps I could understand a little of how they may have felt. I was numb.

When it was over and I went back home, I tried to 'pull myself together' and get on with life, but inside I was crying great sobs of uncontrollable grief and mourned for my lost baby. I would never know the joy of holding him.

During those critical weeks, John had formed a relationship with someone else whom he wanted to marry, so any reconciliation was now not possible. I remained living in my home caring for the boys and Peter would visit and support us in whatever way he could.

Who touched Me?

It was only after I had become a Christian that I could even begin to talk about the incident, and only when I had received the forgiveness of Jesus and the love of Jesus, that I was set free of the sin and guilt and able to forgive myself.

While writing this book, the Holy Spirit has also shown me that I needed to recognise that the ultimate decision to have an abortion, was mine. I had actually been blaming others for not supporting and helping me in the way that I had wanted. As I asked God for His forgiveness, I saw my very small but perfect son lying in the palm of my hand. The root of my sin had been finally dealt with and the Lord had given me the desire of my heart. I was able to hold him.

I know that my baby son, Benjamin, is with the Lord in heaven and one day we shall be re-united. All the years of regret will be turned into an eternity of joy.

The Bible clearly tells us that all babies are united in death to their Creator.

> *'Then his servants said to him* [speaking to David who had just lost his baby son], *"What is this that you have done? You fasted and wept for the child while he was alive, but when the child died, you arose and ate food." So he said, "While the child was still alive, I fasted and wept; for I said, 'Who can tell whether the LORD will be gracious to me, that the child may live?' But now he is dead; why should I fast?*

> *Can I bring him back again? I shall go to him, but he shall
> not return to me.'' '*   (2 Samuel 12:21–23)

David knew his son was with the Lord and that one day he
would see him again.

I have prayed that the Lord will use my experience to help
others and to show that abortion is never an easy option
however difficult the circumstances.

I know one day God will answer my prayer.

For Benjamin and all babies who have died either through miscarriage, stillbirth, infant death or abortion:

In the arms of Jesus,
I know my baby lies,
And somehow, 'though it's hard to bear,
It brings me comfort, knowing there,
My baby never cries.

He'll never know suffering,
Sickness or pain,
Just the joy that heaven brings,
Lullabies the angel sings,
Will be his sweet refrain.

In the arms of Jesus,
My baby now is safe,
And so he'll grow and be complete,
A perfect person when we meet,
In that glorious place.

In the arms of Jesus,
I know I will be one day,
Re-united, precious dear,
And Our Saviour, every tear,
He'll gently wipe away.

Chapter 4

Sickness Strikes
and M.E. Takes its Hold

'I am not at ease, nor am I quiet;
I have no rest, for trouble comes.'
(Job 3:26)

For many years I was an active member of a well-known amateur company who produced some of the most famous musicals, *South Pacific*, *Oliver*, *Kiss Me Kate*, *Oklahoma!*, *Carousel*, *West Side Story*, and many more. To take part in these shows was demanding, physically exhausting at times, but very exciting and tremendous fun. It was while I was rehearsing a technically difficult lift during a dance routine, that I fell and sustained a serious head injury. Not only was this to prove to be the end of my theatrical pursuits, but also the beginning of many weeks of living in a 'closed' world, as the internal bruising took time to heal. I was at this time, working as a teacher at a nursery school, but because of my accident, was absent for many months. When I did return to teaching, I found it very difficult and tiring. The noise of the children was proving to be a real problem and concentration was a major effort. I had only been back at work a short time, when yet another disaster struck.

It was our half-term school holiday, and both Matthew and Daniel were spending their break with their father. The

Hello Dolly *at the Malvern Theatre*

relationship between John and me at this time was particularly bitter. He was divorcing me and preparing to marry someone else. Peter had moved in with us. I was at home on my own and glad of a few days break. It was a very windy day and as I was doing my housework, I was conscious of the wind howling outside. I was standing in my dining room, and as I looked out of my window, to my horror I could see six-foot flames coming from one of the bedrooms. Immediately my body went into overdrive. I picked up the 'phone to dial 999. How long the fire had been blazing was hard to tell, but because of the high winds, it had spread quickly. The fire brigade arrived and with great skill the firemen took control of the situation, although it was five hours before the flames were extinguished.

We were homeless. The fire had completely destroyed the roof and top floor of the house. The black smoke, water and fumes had also ruined the ground floor. The boys arrived home to yet another shock. We had lost most of our clothes and personal possessions. We decided to move in temporarily with Uncle Jack while we took stock of our situation. A few days later I started to look for other accommodation and eventually a friend allowed us to rent her cottage for three months. During this time the boys had chicken-pox, I discovered lumps under my arms and finally Peter and I were married.

On reflection, it was emotionally very sad for us all, but particularly for the boys, who had to make some drastic changes in their lives. Suddenly they had to grow up quickly, adjusting to a new home, new stepfather, and a mother who was always tired.

The lumps I had discovered were worrying me. I had a lump removed from my breast and had several cancer scares. My doctor, while sympathetic, could not offer any real diagnosis. I felt so tired and I knew that my body was sick. I was trying to hold down my job, which was proving to be difficult. I then suffered from an attack of a 'flu-like virus which left me weak and although I struggled back to work, it was becoming more and more apparent to me that there was something seriously wrong. I returned to my doctor, but again, after routine blood tests, nothing positive was diagnosed. The doctor soon took the attitude that there was nothing physically wrong with me, and all I was suffering from was stress and nervous exhaustion.

I kept working, having a few weeks off when it became too much for me, and then returning to school until exhaustion took its toll and once again I would have to return to bed. The lease from the cottage had expired, and so alternative accommodation had to be found once again. Our own home was being rebuilt and we had decided that we would make that our permanent home as soon as it had been completed. Meanwhile, we moved into a large house nearer to Worcester.

It was to be a very unhappy time for us all, with relationships strained once more. It was obvious that in spite of the love that Peter and I had for one another, it was not going to work and so we separated. We had only been married for twenty-one months. Peter left and returned to live with his sister and brother-in-law.

At about this time my uncle Jack had a stroke and was admitted to hospital. I was able to care for him and was with him when he died. My mother, who was also ill, was staying with me.

I found it increasingly more and more difficult to cope as I became weaker and weaker. I was spending more time off sick than actually working, and although the staff and headmistress were supportive and sympathetic, I began to realise that I was becoming too ill to continue. I was very concerned that the boys would now have to leave school, as I would not be earning a sufficient amount of money to pay for their fees. I then discovered that uncle Jack had left me a legacy that not only would cover this need, but also allowed me to purchase my share of the home from Peter. Eventually, when all the money had gone, both boys were granted an assisted place until they left school two years later for University.

One of the most distressing aspects of my illness was the failure to get a diagnosis and to be taken seriously. On each visit to the doctor, I was now treated abruptly and told to take anti-depressants. I had begun to suffer from terrible insomnia, and because of the nature of my job, eventually agreed to take sleeping pills. I was prescribed a drug called Temazepam. The side-effects from taking this drug in my case were vivid dreams, nightmares, forgetfulness and confusion. I did not realise and certainly was not informed of the dangers of taking such a drug long term. Consequently, I became addicted to it. I would suddenly be gripped with the most terrible fear and have panic attacks. These were unpredictable and would happen anywhere. They were beyond my control and would strike at any time. They were totally irrational and very frightening. Unless you have suffered from them yourself, you could never comprehend the devastation they cause. You begin to think you are losing your mind. You are certainly not in control of your body any more.

About this time, I was also experiencing sudden bursts of a rapid heartbeat. They seemed to go out of control, beating up to 140 beats per minute. This made me feel weak and light-headed. The first time this happened, I was taken to hospital and monitored, but sent home once my heart rate had returned to normal. This problem was to continue for months, and again was a very frightening time. My doctor eventually advised me to seek advice from a psychiatrist. I wondered how ill I had to become before I would be taken seriously, but if this was the course I had to take, then I was prepared to take it.

However, although sympathetic to my illness, the psychiatrist could not offer any advice or help. I was beginning to appear to be a baffling case.

I was very unhappy with my doctor's attitude, and so I decided to find another practice. Thankfully, I found a doctor who was not only sympathetic, but also kind and very supportive. For the first time, I was taken seriously. Many tests were carried out and my doctor acknowledged that there was something seriously wrong with me.

I began to read in the newspapers, reports of people suffering from very similar symptoms to the ones I was experiencing. Usually, the onset of this mysterious illness began with 'flu-like symptoms, that would leave its patients with extreme exhaustion, from which they never completely recovered. Rest seemed to be the only answer, which could be for many days, or in my case, weeks. Then there may be a time of respite when you felt as if you might recover. However, as soon as you tried to do the normal basic things, you would end up feeling very weak and have to return to your bed. It was interesting to find out that as many as 150,000 people were sufferers of this disease. One of the great frustrations for the sufferers was not to be taken seriously. This was a real physical disease and not psychosomatic. The disease was called Myalgic Encephalomyelitis, or M.E. for short.

I discussed my thoughts and feelings concerning the possibility that indeed I might be suffering from this with my doctor. He was quite happy for me to pursue further advice, to see if indeed I could get a definite diagnosis. One of the main problems with this illness is that it is a very difficult disease to diagnose. Nothing positive can be found in blood tests, or the usual type of tests that are carried out for diagnosing known diseases. I had months of checking my own blood count, with no positive results. I then heard of a specialist, working in the research of M.E., and so it was arranged for him to visit me in my home. This he did, and after a long talk discussing my symptoms, he came to the conclusion that I indeed was a chronic sufferer of M.E. (see medical letter on pp. 9–10).

I felt such a relief to at last to be able to put a name to my illness. I felt that now, perhaps I would be taken seriously and not be treated as a hypochondriac. (Since writing this book, I am glad to say that much research has been done and early recognition of M.E. is now possible. Early diagnosis and rest can prevent the condition from becoming chronic.)

It was decided that I would consult a specialist in London, who may be able to help me with my diet. I went to St Bartholomew's Hospital and underwent more tests. I had an EMG to test muscle function. The results led the consultant to confirm the diagnosis. I also had a brain scan, but thankfully, no abnormality was found. At this stage, I was struggling with extreme exhaustion, muscular twitching and pains, intolerance to light, inability to concentrate or hold a conversation, sensitivity to noise, chronic insomnia and had developed oral thrush. I had become allergic to many foods and was advised to keep to a very strict diet to combat Candida Albicans. The treatment was to include a course of injections known as Enzyme Potentiated Desensitisation to help the food allergies, nystatin, fungilin and a course of Germanium. Not only was it a great ordeal to have to travel to London for this treatment, but also it was extremely expensive. However, when your health is taken away from you, you will try anything and everything if there is a remote chance that it might work.

Consuming many vitamin supplements also played a big part in the intense regime to try and restore my health. At one time, I was taking a daily cocktail of over twenty-five different tablets. I have often reflected upon the effect that all these tablets must have had on my body, and when I was told to stop taking Germanium powders because the United States of America had banned the drug due to fears from possible carcinogenic repercussions, perhaps more harm that good was achieved. I had spent a vast amount of money, and felt no better.

So, here I was, confined mainly to bed, very weak and thin, financially much worse off, and with no hope of any real improvement in my condition. On reflection, I suppose it would have been easy to let depression get its hold, but somehow thankfully this never happened. I had the boys to consider, and I knew that I had to keep going for their sakes. I did ring the Samaritans, but suicide was not on my mind.

My eating habits were becoming an increasing problem. I had lost all pleasure in food and now began to think that I was unable to eat. The very thought of food made me retch.

The warning bells rang, and I suddenly realised that if I was not careful I could become anorexic. I made the decision to force the food down. It had been quite a battle. I weighed 5 stone 11 lbs.

Who touched me?

Eating disorders affect millions of people. But there is hope and help available. There are various organisations that can be of great value. One of those is Swansea City Mission (incorporating the former Kainos Trust).

Kainos Trust for eating disorders was an affiliated organisation of the Association of Christian Counsellors. The Founder and Director was Helena Wilkinson. Helena nearly died from anorexia as a teenager. However, whilst she was in hospital at the age of 16, a Christian lady who was on the same ward had a prophetic word for Helena; that she would come through the anorexia knowing Jesus, that her name would be in print and that she would be well known for having overcome anorexia.

When Helena was 18 years old she became a committed Christian and subsequently overcame anorexia. During this time she wrote an autobiographical book *Puppet on a String*. As a result she was inundated with desperate cries for help from people with eating disorders.

Helena went on to train in counselling, write other books on various subjects and lecture internationally on eating disorders. Around ten years later she founded Kainos Trust. On 1 January 2004 Kainos Trust joined forces with Swansea City Mission with all activities coming under Nicholaston House:

    Nicholaston House
    Penmaen, Gower
    Swansea SA3 2HL

Since writing this book, I have experienced the healing touch of Jesus in many areas of my life. Jesus ultimately is the one who can rescue and restore even the most hopeless of cases. Nothing is impossible for Him. When you become one of His children, as you learn to bring to Him your pain, broken relationships, fears and heartaches, He will gently lift from your shoulders even the most painful memory and heaviest burden and replace them with His healing love. It can often be a long hard road, but with Jesus it is a road of recovery.

Weary Traveller

I am a weary traveller who has walked along life's way,
And on my back is a bag of stones I have collected day
    by day.
The first ones were placed there when I was still quite
    small
In childhood days, with rejection and self-pity I recall.
Then bitterness, a bigger stone, was put upon my back
Selfishness, self-centredness, were things I didn't lack
And as I grew I came across more for my collection,
Unforgiveness, jealousy and even more rejection.
And if you think that was enough and perhaps no more
    I'd find
I turned the corner and there would be lust of every kind.
Next, the stone of covetousness, and its partner greed
Resentment and rudeness were ones I didn't need
But because of lack of self-control I grabbed them one
    by one
And quickly put them into place as my other friends
    had done.
Then anger appeared and stubbornness his friend
Pride, greed then heartache, oh! there seemed to be no end.
Then finally, betrayal, such a heavy rock
Yet still I stooped to pick it up, but fell as if in shock.
So I sat upon the roadside and there alone I cried
When suddenly, I noticed someone standing at my side.
I ceased to shake as I gazed into His gentle eyes,
He smiled, took my hand and then to my surprise
He told me He had followed me and knew me very well.
How this could be I did not know, but He began to tell
That He was there for all who truly search and seek.
Why had it taken me so long this man to finally meet?
'You were blind and could not see,' He began to softly say.
'Why didn't you stop me and take my scales away?'

'Your freedom, not captivity is My Father's will
You must recognise your need and then I can fulfil
All your heart's desire as you turn and follow Me.'
It all seemed so simple as He spoke explicitly
'Come with your burdens, and I will give you rest'
And then He did something I never would have guessed.
One by one He took the stones, gently from my back
Until all were gone and I was left with just an empty sack.
I held my head and stood up tall for the first time in my life
I felt love and peace and joy in place of anguish and strife
And isn't it beautiful that this message for today
Is for all mankind who tread along life's troubled way.
So if you have never met Him, yet yearn to be set free,
Come, bring all your stones to the feet at Calvary.

Chapter 5

Mountain of Joy
and Valley of Grief

'Therefore, if anyone is in Christ,
he is a new creation;
old things have passed away;
behold all things have become new.'
(2 Corinthians 5:17)

It was 8th November 1988, the morning after I had asked the Lord into my life. I felt different in every way, peaceful and calm. Something had happened to me deep down inside of me. It is hard to explain, but in many ways I felt as if it was the beginning of a new life. Everything seemed new. I felt as if my past burdens had been taken from me. It was as if Jesus had lifted all my pains and sufferings, physical, mental and emotional, and in their place, given me rest. I was lying in my bed wallowing in His presence, knowing that He was in control of my destiny, and somehow it did not matter what happened to me in my circumstances; my trust and hope were in Him.

I had decided not to say too much to the boys at this stage, but I am sure they must have noticed a difference in me. I was, however, very anxious to share my experience with my mother. I knew that she was very worried about me and must have felt helpless, as her health was deteriorating and she was now spending her time in and out of hospital. Her heart was weakening, and although she never complained, she must have realised that she was dying. She had a terrible fear of dying in hospital, and her only wish was that she would be allowed to die in her own bed. One of my greatest regrets, was that I was unable to look after her. Because of my own illness, I was only able to visit her three times during her many weeks in hospital. Peter had been a tremendous support to her, taking over the care and concern in my place. He visited her every day, taking in little sandwiches and cream cakes, which she loved. It was a special time for both of them, and I know they cared about each other very much.

I prayed that I would be strong enough to see her, and it was arranged that Peter would come and collect me and take me to the hospital at the end of that week. I had time to rest, reflect and seek God.

As I lay on my bed in the stillness and quietness of the morning, I wondered if I could still pray in the heavenly language as I had done before. I wondered what I should do. Perhaps it only happened yesterday, and that I would not experience it again. I felt sad and hoped that was not the case. I was still a little apprehensive, because I knew this was something supernatural, wonderful, but beyond human logic or comprehension. I began to speak to Jesus and sing to Him, praising Him for coming into my life. As I was doing this, I began once again to whisper those beautiful words. I was so happy! I knew that this gift, which had been given to me, would never leave me.

To pray in tongues, so-called because there are many different tongues, brings a wonderful release of praying in the spirit. Sometimes, when I have felt too weak to pray, or have simply not felt like praying, to pray in this manner, lifts you above your circumstances and enables you to communicate with the Lord in a truly wonderful way.

'But God has revealed them to us through His Spirit. For the
Spirit searches all things, yes, the deep things of God. For
what man knows the things of a man except the spirit of the
man which is in him? Even so no one knows the things of God
except the Spirit of God. Now we have received, not the spirit
of the world, but the Spirit who is from God, that we might
know the things that have been freely given to us by God.
These things we also speak, not in words which man's
wisdom teaches but which the Holy Spirit teaches, comparing
spiritual things with spiritual. But the natural man does not
receive the things of the Spirit of God, for they are foolishness
to him; nor can he know them, because they are spiritually
discerned.' (1 Corinthians 2:10–14)

Every time I thought about Jesus, my stomach turned
over. It was the same experience that I had felt when 'falling
in love', the excitement and nervousness, both emotions felt
at the same time. Only this time, it was different, for the
person I was falling in love with was Jesus! I would never
have thought that was possible, had it not happened to me.
My love for Him has deepened over the years, as the Holy
Spirit has revealed more of Jesus to me. Most precious of all is
that nothing can come between this love that will go on for
all eternity.

'For I am persuaded that neither death nor life, nor angels nor
principalities nor powers, nor things present nor things to
come, nor height nor depth, nor any other created thing, shall
be able to separate us from the love of God which is in Christ
Jesus our Lord.' (Romans 8:38–39)

The end of the week arrived and Peter came to collect me
to take me to the hospital. I was carried into the car and
pushed in my wheelchair to the ward. My mother was sitting
propped up in her bed. Her face lit up as she saw me. There

seemed so much to say, and I wanted to be sure that I did not miss anything out! She listened with interest and was very pleased about my apparent discovery of inner happiness. She confessed that she seemed to have lost all her faith, but was very glad that I had had this experience. I kissed her and came home. I knew that it would take me several days to recuperate from the visit, but I was so thankful that I had been able to see her.

Several weeks later, I was able to visit her again. What a precious time we had together. She shared with me and told me things that she had never said before. We talked about loving each other and she told me how special I was to her. It seemed all barriers had been broken down and we were just left with an overwhelming love for one another. Although we often spoke on the telephone after that special time, I never saw her again. The day she was allowed to come home from hospital, her very first night in her own bed, she died.

God had granted her wish, and had not taken her until she had come home. How I needed the Lord to help me through this difficult time. I had lost my best friend, but then of course Jesus knew all this. He knew how much I would need Him. I believe that such was the grief, that without the supernatural peace that was now in my heart. I would have 'given up' and died too. All I knew was that I was being carried through it all, and although I was not able to go to her funeral, I was able to cope with many of the arrangements. Our local vicar was away, so another vicar had taken over his duties.

As far as I was concerned this again was another gift from the Lord, for He sent me a gentle vicar, who loved the Lord as I now did, who prayed in 'tongues'. What more could I have asked for? I had never heard of a 'born again' Christian, never met one before Linda and Claire had visited me, and now the Lord had sent me one of His servants to conduct my mother's funeral. My friends told me that it was a beautiful service and I am sure that it was.

I have often wondered about my mother, whether or not she is with the Lord. I knew that since my conversion, no one could get to heaven unless they have been saved. I knew my mother was a believer, but I also knew that was not enough.

Over a period of time, I believe the Lord has shown me that she is with Him. I believe that my testimony to her shortly before she died was enough for her to cry out to Him for her salvation, and of course He was there for her.

I had been a Christian for just over four weeks. Linda and Claire came to visit me once or twice to pray and encourage me. I knew that this was very beneficial to me, but I am not so sure about the boys. Understandably I expect they found some of the things quite difficult to comprehend. I am sure I would have felt the same had I been in their position. I am afraid I did not help matters and constantly 'Bible bashed' them in my anxiety to get them to make a decision to follow Christ. I have since learnt to trust God with their lives, to love them for who they are unconditionally and to uplift them in prayer.

Who touched Me?

The Lord has since shown me the need to forgive my mother for the many things that hurt me. One specific time was when she left me in Hampshire and took my sister back with her to Worcester. I felt she had abandoned me. Forgiving her in the name of Jesus, brought tears of sadness, then a release as He healed the pain of so long ago.

I believe the Lord wants to minister to you. This is one of the reasons you are reading this book. Ask Him to show you the areas in your past where He can touch you too.

Chapter 6

Valley of Pain

'Yea, though I walk through the valley of the shadow of death,
I will fear no evil;
For You are with me;
Your rod and Your staff, they comfort me.'
(Psalm 23:4)

As winter turned to spring, I began to enjoy a few days of better health. I was able to drive into town and collect the boys from school. This was a great joy to me and although it was only short lived, it was such a thrill to be able to see the countryside, smell the fresh air and begin to appreciate the things of life we so often take for granted.

It was during this time of 'remission' that I decided to have a check-up with my doctor. I had had gynaecological problems in the past and I was concerned not to neglect what I considered would be a routine examination. It was a complete surprise to me when I was told that I must see a specialist without delay. A few days later, I found myself attending a clinic at the local hospital. It was another shock to be told that I must have a hysterectomy as quickly as possible. I felt numb. The thought of having to face major surgery with M.E. knowing that even the anaesthetic would have a distressing and debilitating effect alone, suddenly left me feeling frightened and drained. I felt mentally as well as physically unprepared for what lay ahead.

I had, or so I thought, a week in which to make all the arrangements. However, what was about to happen next was quite unexpected. God often intervenes, and I am sure that this was His way of letting Him take care of all the details, which would have drained what little strength I had left.

I woke up very early the next morning, with the most excruciating pain in my right side. I had had this pain before, but this was so acute that it sent my body into shock. A cold sweat swept over me and my heartbeat became very slow and laboured. I called for Matthew to come to me. He appeared at the door, and one look on his face was enough for both of us to realise the seriousness of the situation. He 'phoned for an ambulance and I was taken to hospital. The specialist, whom I had begun to look upon as a very caring man, came to see me and to put my mind at rest, by assuring me that I would be carefully monitored and a decision would be made as to when to operate. It had been hoped that because of my poor physical condition, I might be able to rest for a few days and so try and build up my strength before the operation; a cyst on one of my ovaries had burst, hence the emergency admission.

So many people were kind and supportive to me. It was a special time when differences in personal relationships were put aside, and everyone tried to help one another. John came down to see me straight away, taking time off work to sort out some of the practical details. My sister-in-law agreed to cook the meals for the boys each evening. They would stay at home on their own during the week, and spend time with their father at the weekends. I had not seen or heard from Peter for nearly two years, but he made contact with me shortly after my operation and came to visit me.

It was decided that I would rest for as long as possible and then I would be transferred to the local private hospital, where the operation would be done. I was so grateful that Peter had still continued to include me in his BUPA policy (private medical care). It was to prove to be such a blessing to me in my many weeks of recovery.

How I needed to hang on to the Lord. I needed His comfort more than ever. The time I had in the local hospital before my transfer was to be a very unhappy one. The sister-in-charge seemed to take an instant dislike to me. She assured me that there was no such thing as M.E. and that I would not get any special treatment. When I wanted to go to the bathroom, I was to walk like everyone else. The bathroom was actually right down the far end of the ward and only those who know what it is to have M.E. will understand the implications of her statement. I could not believe that anyone who is in charge of a ward of patients, who often feel vulnerable and frightened, would behave in this manner. It was a nightmare. I was so glad when John spoke to the specialist who then told the sister that I was to have a chair to take me to the bathroom. From that moment on, she totally ignored me.

The pain kept sweeping over me in waves. Each time this happened, I instinctively placed my hands over my stomach and prayed quietly in tongues. What blessed assurance to know that in spite of everything, He was with me. To come against such ignorance at a time when I felt so low, seemed to be the final blow. Because I knew Jesus, in His strength I was able to forgive the sister and rise up above the situation. Hallelujah!

During my brief stay in that ward, I had a visit from John's wife, whom I had never met before. She had come down without John's knowledge, sending a little note via a nurse to ask if she could come and see me. It was a precious time and I thought she was a very caring person. I was so grateful that she did not mind me borrowing John during this crisis.

I was feeling emotionally drained and physically very weak. How I longed for my mother. As I lay trying to sleep in the open ward, I began to think about what might happen to me. In spite of the circumstances, I felt relaxed and calm. As I was drifting off to sleep, I heard quite clearly a voice in my head saying,

'Gillian, you are going to be all right, because I am going to be with you.'

I held my breath as I realised that it must be God speaking to me. No one ever called me by my full Christian name other than my mother, brother and sister. I was known as Gill, or Gillie, I was not used to being called Gillian. This was divine confirmation, and just given to me at a time when I needed it most. I went to sleep ready to climb the mountain that lay before me. Jesus would be climbing it with me.

Two days later, I was transferred to the private hospital. I was so grateful for the peace and quiet of my own room. My bed was opposite a large window and just outside, growing in the garden was a beautiful tree. I was soon to learn that every day, squirrels would come gathering whatever they could find and chase up and down the lawns. For the weeks I spent in my room, watching these delightful creatures brought me much joy. Alone in my little room, I was to have such wonderful times with Him. Such closeness that I never wanted it to end; my mountain became a rich blessing for me. I learned so much about His forgiveness, His faithfulness and His unconditional love. That closeness has never left me. It has just led my walk with Him into richer fields.

On the morning of the operation, John came and stayed with me. I asked him to read Psalm 121:

'I will lift up my eyes to the hills –
From whence comes my help?
My help comes from the LORD,
Who made heaven and earth.

He will not allow your foot to be moved;
He who keeps you will not slumber.
Behold, He who keeps Israel
Shall neither slumber nor sleep.

The LORD is your keeper,
The LORD is your shade at your right hand.
The sun shall not strike you by day,
Nor the moon by night.

The LORD shall preserve you from all evil;
He shall preserve your soul.
The LORD shall preserve your going out
    and your coming in
From this time forth, and even evermore.'

I was asked if I would like to have a pre-med to help me relax. I had had these before, and certainly they had a calming effect and could be very beneficial, especially if you were apprehensive.

'No thank you!' was my reply. 'I have the Lord and that is enough.' I knew that if I woke up in heaven that would be wonderful, and if I woke up in bed that would be wonderful as well!

I remember coming round from surgery and feeling as if I had been run over by a steamroller. I had an oxygen mask on my face and I was closely monitored through the night. The nursing staff were very caring and sympathetic, not only because I had just had an operation, but they could see that I was very ill with M.E. The first few days were a blur to me. Unfortunately I developed a urinary infection and began passing blood. In spite of several courses of antibiotics I had to return again later for minor surgery to correct this problem. It was during this slow and painful recovery from surgery, that I had a vision of the Lord.

One morning, I was in the bathroom feeling faint from acute pain. I was praying quietly in tongues because that was all I could do. I was crying to the Lord, when I was suddenly aware of a figure sitting beside me. The figure was dressed in a long shining white robe.

It was only there for a few seconds, but such was the peace that I knew I was standing on Holy ground. I know that in that brief moment of time I had been a witness to an angel? Or was it Jesus? But one thing was clear, I had felt the presence of God. My heavenly Father was telling me that we were going through this together. My pain was His pain, my heartache was His heartache. His promise in His word was the truth.

'... I will not leave you nor forsake you.' (Joshua 1:5)

I thank God that He allowed me the privilege of that moment, and has since on other occasions revealed fleeting moments of heaven itself. How glad I am that I said 'Yes!' to His invitation. He took me just as I was, gave me a new life and made me feel beautiful.

Three weeks later I went home.

Chapter 7

My Miracle of Healing

'... If only I may touch His garment, I shall be made well.'
(Matthew 9:21)

What joy to be back in my own home! I could hardly believe how weak I had become, but I knew that with His help, I would be able to cope. Matthew and Daniel had decided to stay for a well-earned break with their father.

The transition from hospital with its constant care and attention to an empty house would again have been very difficult without the knowledge of my Father's love for me. I learnt to rely on Him for everything and He always provided for my needs. I continued to have support from the home help service, although their time was always limited. I also had private help several times a week. Again, I will always be grateful for the care these ladies gave me.

Gradually over the weeks I became stronger, although I was still battling with the symptoms of M.E. I continued with my strict diet, took my many pills and went to London for treatment.

During these months, I had some wonderful times with the Lord. I had grown hungry for His Word and loved the stillness and quietness I felt in His presence. I had learnt that only when you are resting and 'being still' can you hear His voice. How sad to think that we can miss so many of these opportunities by being pre-occupied with other things. I would like to share some of those supernatural revelations that I experienced with you.

A particularly difficult aspect of my illness, was when I was suffering from acute intolerance to daylight. I would have to spend my time lying in bed with the curtains drawn, as any glimmer of light caused extreme pain. A darkened bedroom was my only respite. Early one morning, after spending a sleepless, painful night, I felt the presence of God in my room. I was very conscience of a brilliant white light. Actually, no words can describe this phenomena. Surely, this must be the white light people often talk about seeing when they are close to death. Was this the glorious light of heaven? When this vision passed and I opened my eyes, I had to close them quickly because of the great pain that was caused by the daylight in my room. Yet, this natural light was nothing in comparison to the light I had just witnessed. It was beautiful.

On another occasion, I woke myself up laughing! I just could not stop myself. Looking at my circumstances, I should be crying! I realised that I was laughing in the Spirit. I felt this deep bubbling inside of me just welling up. It was an acute attack of the giggles. It brought a great feeling of well-being. I think everyone will agree that laughing is a wonderful exercise. It has happened to me on several occasions.

Another experience which had a profound effect upon me, happened one day during a brief time of remission. I was driving my car to fetch the boys from school. As I was waiting at the traffic lights, I noticed a woman pushing a pram. I was suddenly flooded with an overwhelming love for her. She was a complete stranger to me and yet, in that moment of time, for a few brief seconds, Jesus allowed me to feel His love that He and our heavenly Father have for the human race. It totally consumed my very being.

Twelve months had passed, and it was summer again. I

would like to say that I was improving, but the truth was, I was getting weaker.

Daniel came regularly to my room, bringing flowers that he had picked from the garden. He would put them in a vase by the side of my bed.

'The garden's really beautiful. I'd like you to be able to see it,' he said. 'I could carry you downstairs and put you in your wheelchair.'

What a lovely thought! It had been many weeks since I was able to venture outside. It was my birthday soon. I decided that my goal would be to make that trip. The day arrived, but I was just too weak to go. However, the day after, Daniel succeeded in carrying me into the garden. I shall never forget the sight of the roses in full bloom, or the intoxicating smell of their perfume. It was the best birthday present I could have wished for. It would be one of those moments that would be etched on to my mind forever.

During this time I had received monthly leaflets which had been posted through my letterbox. They were invitations to a 'Praise and worship' evening at the local village hall. I could tell by the leaflets that these people were Christians who loved the Lord as I did. I made up my mind that one evening I would go. The months ticked by, but eventually the day arrived when I knew that I would be given the strength to attend. The meeting started at 7.30 p.m. Daniel took me to the hall in the car and arranged to collect me after 30 minutes. I knew that I would not be able to stay for very long, but was excited about being in the company of other Christians. As soon as I entered the hall, I was over-whelmed by the welcome and love shown to me and although my time with them was over too quickly, I returned home knowing that I had been in the presence of God. Little did I realise then, but this church, St Paul's Church, and these people would become part of my life in a way that I would never have thought possible.

During the spring and summer of 1990, I struggled even to maintain any quality of life. I would be carried downstairs, only to be able to spend a couple of hours on the settee before having to return to my bed. I was becoming very weak and tired, and I had begun to feel as if I was losing the will to live. I had fought this illness for so long, and I had now become weary. I had begun to think in my own mind, that perhaps the time had come for me to go and be with the Lord. I had remembered praying and asking the Lord if I could be around for the boys at least until they had left school. Matthew had just completed his A-levels and Daniel his GCSEs (school examinations). Maybe this was the time for Him to take me home. One of my greatest fears, was wondering how the boys would cope if they found that I had died during the night. Even breathing had become difficult and would take up all my energy. I put my face into the pillow and whispered a prayer.

'Jesus, I have nothing left to fight this disease any longer. It is up to You now to help me.'

I knew my only hope and help would have to come from Him. As I lay in the stillness of my room, I suddenly felt a desire to switch on my television, something that I had not done for a very long time. As soon as I did this, I understood why, for I was watching a programme about the work that Jackie Pullinger was doing for the Lord in the walled city in Hong Kong (read *Chase the Dragon*). The power of the Holy Spirit was transforming the lives of many of the worst drug addicts as they came to Christ. Jackie and her helpers would sit by them and pray over them in 'tongues'. I knew that the Lord was prompting me to start to use this gift, which I had neglected due to my weakness. I closed my eyes and began to pray quietly in the heavenly language. As I began to do this, I felt the power of the Lord come upon me and I continued to pray in this way for some time.

> 'For he who speaks in a tongue does not speak to men but to
> God ... '   (1 Corinthians 14:2)

My spirit was speaking directly to my heavenly Father.

For many years I had been receiving a severe disablement
allowance, which had helped me financially. Each year, a
different doctor would assess my degree of immobility. This
experience would often leave me exhausted once again and
I would have to have many days of bed rest in order to
recuperate. The time had arrived for my annual assessment.
The last thing I felt I could cope with was this ordeal.
However, although Matthew had tried to postpone the date,
the doctor explained that it would be necessary for him to
visit otherwise my pension would be affected. When he
arrived, Matthew brought him to my bedroom and stayed
with me in order to answer any questions on my behalf and
so eliminating any unnecessary exertion. The doctor sat on a
chair at the end of my bed and began to take notes. He
seemed a gentle and caring man and showed concern for my
situation.

I turned to him and asked, 'Do you know of anything at all
that can help people like me?'

He put down his pad and replied,

'Yes, **Jesus Christ can heal you.**'

I will never be able to put into words how I felt at that
moment, but all I knew was that God had sent him. Only the
Lord could have heard my recent cry from my heart, and
now this doctor was telling me that Jesus could heal me!

Dr Peter Quinton prayed for me and as he did, my faith
rose, the peace of the Lord consumed me and I knew in my
heart that I would recover. Before he left, he shared a little of
the Lord's divine power, as he had been led over the years to
pray for many sick and dying patients who had recovered.
After he had gone, I placed my Prothiaden tablets, which I

had been taking since my mother's death, in a drawer. I was now going to fix my eyes on Jesus. The date was Friday, 29 June 1990.

It was interesting to learn later, that in fact my severe disablement allowance had been granted until the year 2023. The medical profession were so sure that my health would never improve that they even decided that I would never need to be assessed again. I had a very frustrating time trying to send back my pay cheques!

The following morning, I had a telephone call from a woman called Gretta. She and her husband Joe, were good friends of Tony and Pat Chamberlain, two of the Christian friends I had met at the village hall. Tony and Pat were missionaries to the Philippines and before they left, they had asked Gretta if she would get in touch with me. She offered to send me some tape recordings of the services that were held at St Paul's Church. I received them gladly, and when I listened, I could hardly believe what I was hearing. A woman was giving her testimony of how the Lord had healed her after she had spent 25 years in a wheelchair! She had been completely healed as she attended a crusade in Birmingham. She now travelled the world sharing what Jesus had done for her. At the end of the tape, she mentioned her friend who travelled with her, and she had been healed of M.E. The Lord was certainly trying to tell me something.

Gretta and Joe came to visit me, and this was to be the first of many visits. They shared their faith, encouraged me and continued to pray for my complete healing. I will always be grateful for their support at this crucial time. Each time they prayed for me, I felt the Lord strengthening my thin weak legs, restoring my health and enabling me to begin to live a normal life again. I knew for certain that every step I took, Jesus was with me. The joy of being able to cook a meal for the boys was such a blessing to me. To be able to make a cake without having to spend days in bed from sheer exhaustion was such bliss. (For many years, Matthew had had a deep problem with his birthday celebrations. He said he hated them and they filled him with dread. This upset me greatly and only recently have I discovered the reason behind this. Apparently, he remembers me having to remain in bed for days after I had got up specifically to make him a birthday cake. It must have been very difficult for both Matthew and Daniel and I expect I shall never fully realize the emotional and psychological pressures they had to face and work through over the years of my illness.)

Each day I was getting stronger. I seemed to be doing so well, and so I was shocked when one morning I woke up to find all the symptoms of M.E. return. I could not understand it, as I knew in my heart that I had been healed. I rang up Joe who came with Gretta to see me. The three of us prayed. The Holy Spirit revealed that I had had a curse put on my life.

Apparently, when my mother was in labour, she asked my father if he would fetch the doctor. (Both my brother and I were home births.) He told her that she would have to wait until he had finished milking the cows! The doctor arrived after I was born – not the most sensitive of situations in which to come into the world. His negative response became a stumbling block to me. Looking back I was very much aware that I had been troubled by ill-health, accidents and many operations, whilst my brother and sister enjoyed good health.

We then prayed and this curse was broken in the name of Jesus. From that moment on I was completely set free. The date was Saturday, 25th August 1990.

Who touched me?

Curses are very real and can be spoken over us by other people. Our parents or teachers may say to us negative words: 'You are no good; you are useless'; 'You will never be clever'; 'Can't you do anything right?'; 'You are always ill', etc. They can also be inherited from our ancestors – known as generational curses – and we can speak curses over our own lives. Read Derek Prince's book *Blessing or Curse: You Can Choose*.

Through the counsel of godly men guided by the Holy Spirit, you too can be set free.

> *'Death and life are in the power of the tongue,*
> *And those who love it will eat its fruit.'*   (Proverbs 18:21)

The good news is that Jesus paid the price for every curse at Calvary:

> *'Christ has redeemed us from the curse of the law, having become a curse for us (for it is written, "Cursed is everyone who hangs on a tree").*   (Galatians 3:13)

Chapter 8

Supernatural Manifestations

'... for the battle is the LORD'S,
and He will give you [Goliath] into our hands.'
(1 Samuel 17:47)

As human beings, we are not always comfortable with things of the supernatural. We feel much happier if we can work things out in our own minds and come up with a valid reason as to why and how things have happened the way they have. We can also take this attitude with us in our Christianity. We can somehow feel more secure in a church, which does not move or accept supernatural experiences. I know that for years I attended churches where there was no movement of the Holy Spirit. I do not ever recall anyone preaching the true gospel message; of our individual need to accept Jesus as our personal Saviour. I never understood that the Holy Spirit is the person who helps us to know Christ and enables us to follow Jesus. It is the Holy Spirit who draws us to Christ after entering our life at conversion. Living the Christian life is impossible without the Holy Spirit. Take the supernatural out of Christianity, and you are left with a dead religion.

Jesus preached many times on hell. The whole purpose of Calvary was to defeat the devil and all the powers of darkness. The cross was a place of victory. Jesus rose victoriously from death and through His shed blood conquered the powers of darkness once and for all.

He paid the price for you and me. It was your sin and mine that put Him there. Jesus went to hell in our place. He knows what hell is like. It is a real place, so terrible that it is beyond description. We, in our own way, often say that some experience we have had or seen in our own lives has been 'worse than hell'. Nothing we experience on this earth is anything like the real place called hell. The greatest tragedy that can happen to any man or woman is for that person to die in their sinful state. Their own sin will send them there, and the blood that Jesus shed for them will be tragically wasted.

Often, before we become Christians, we may not even believe that there is a devil, or at least treat him as some sort of joke. We realise that this is far from the truth once we belong to God. For while you belong to the devil he will not bother you, but once you have made your stand for Jesus Christ, you will become aware of an opposition. The good news is to remember some simple facts that Jesus has told us; God has provided for us our spiritual armour.

'Finally, my brethren, be strong in the Lord and in the power of His might. Put on the whole armour of God, that you may be able to stand against the wiles of the devil. For we do not wrestle against flesh and blood, but against principalities, against powers, against the rulers of the darkness of this age, against spiritual hosts of wickedness in the heavenly places. Therefore take up the whole armour of God, that you may be able to withstand in the evil day, and having done all, to stand. Stand therefore, having girded your waist with truth, having on the breastplate of righteousness, and having shod your feet with the preparation of the gospel of peace; above all, taking the shield of faith with which you will be able to quench all the fiery darts of the wicked one. And take the

helmet of salvation, and the sword of the Spirit, which is the
word of God.'   (Ephesians 6:10–17)

Satan has been defeated and we have the victory.

'But thanks be to God, who gives us the victory through our
Lord Jesus Christ.'   (1 Corinthians 15:57)

I know what it is like to be in the midst of a demonic battle
and am very much aware of demonic attacks. I have had
'hands' pulling me out of bed, trying to choke me, the
feeling of a great pressure on my chest and having to fight
for my very breath. I have had out of body experiences when
I have been fighting to return to my body as it lay on the bed.
I have heard voices speaking to me and seen spiritual beings
in my room. I have sensed the most awful presence of fear.
The powers of evil are very real. But this is the most exciting
thing that I can testify: that in the name of Jesus, all demons
must flee. I have proved the power of the words in the
Scriptures through my own experiences. I have often lain
there and spoken out a scripture, taking authority over the
powers of darkness in the name of Jesus ... and the demons
have gone.

On the cross Jesus completely overcame all the powers of
darkness for us. In Colossians 2:14 Paul reminds us of one
of Satan's weapons that Jesus has taken out of the way
(the accusations arising from the regulations prescribed
by the Mosaic law), having nailed it to the cross. We then
read:

'Having disarmed principalities and powers, He [Jesus] *made*
a public spectacle of them, triumphing over them in it.'

(Colossians 2:15)

There is total victory in the cross.

Sometimes I have been awake during these attacks, but physically paralysed, unable to speak. I have just thought the name of Jesus, and 'they' have gone.

We have nothing to fear once we belong to the Lord. Do not let the devil rob you of your joy. When you feel oppressed, or you or your family are under attack, remember to stand against him. God's Word tells us *'resist the devil and he **will** flee from you!'*; not that he might think about it or that he may, but that he **will**. He has to because of the blood of Jesus.

> *'Therefore submit to God. Resist the devil and he will flee from you.'* (James 4:7)

The most common area of attack can be in the mind. Again the Bible tells us to be alert:

> *'Be sober, be vigilant; because your adversary the devil walks about like roaring lion, seeking whom he may devour. Resist him, steadfast in the faith ... '* (1 Peter 5:8–9)

Any thoughts that are destructive or condemning are from the devil. For he has come to kill, steal and destroy. Recognise these areas and stand against them in Jesus' name! There is no need to be afraid.

> *'For God has not given us a spirit of fear, but of power and of love and a sound mind.'* (2 Timothy 1:7)

And do not forget, we all have thoughts that are offensive, thoughts of temptation; even Jesus was tempted by the devil (Luke 4:1–13). But temptation only becomes sin when we give into it. Think and dwell on the good things.

> *'Finally, brethren whatever things are true, whatever things are noble, whatever things are just, whatever things are pure,*

> *whatever things are lovely, whatever things are of good report,
> if there is any virtue and if there is anything praiseworthy –
> meditate on these things.'* (Philippians 4:8)

Ask the Lord to give you a deeper understanding of the power that is in the blood of Jesus. For that very same power that was released 2,000 years ago is available through His blood today. Learn by heart all the scriptures about the blood.

> *'But now in Christ Jesus you who once were far off have been
> made near by the blood of Christ.'* (Ephesians 2:13)

> *'And they overcame him by the blood of the Lamb and by the
> word of their testimony, and they did not love their lives to
> the death.'* (Revelation 12:11)

Ask the Holy Spirit to help you begin to recognise the attacks from the enemy, as they can take many forms. They can come through your circumstances, finances, family and loved ones, especially those you are perhaps praying for. Physical sickness can also sometimes be demonic, but remember that

> *'... He who is in you is greater than he who is in the world.'*
> (1 John 4:4)

Let us learn from our experiences to be on guard, and to praise God for the victory. To be good and faithful warriors and fight the fight:

> *'... we are more than conquerors through Him who loved us.'*
> (Romans 8:37)

So onward Christian soldiers, let us keep our eyes fixed on Jesus, stand on His Word, rejoice in His promises and remember that nothing can separate us from the love of God.

'Bronwyn' and me after I was healed

After I was healed, one of the first things I did was to take my little dog, Bronwyn, for a walk. She had been my loyal companion during the latter part of my illness. I thought I had been selfish to have another dog after I had lost my previous border terrier, as my future was then uncertain. But the Lord knew that one day I would be able to take her for real walks.

So my dream became a reality. To be able to walk in the beautiful countryside, to smell the fresh air, to drink in the colours of nature around me and most wonderful of all, to be able to praise the Creator

Who touched me?

If you are not yet a Christian, you may have found this chapter difficult to understand, or it may even have disturbed you. I did not understand it either until I had asked Jesus into my life. He showed me that we do not have to be afraid. For He sets us free from our fears and gives us an abundant life.

He will do the same for you.

PART TWO

Chapter 9

Set Free to Serve

'And you shall know the truth,
and the truth shall make you free.'
(John 8:32)

I now had to alter my whole way of thinking. I felt as if I had been in prison and now I had been set free! It was not easy during those first few weeks of acting out my faith and 'proving' my healing. Doubts still flooded my mind, and that annoying voice in my head was always telling me that if I pushed myself I would have a relapse. I recognised how deceptive the devil can be, trying to put these fears into my mind, but I knew in my heart that Jesus had healed me and no one was going to rob me of that victory. I knew that for each step of faith I took, He would be with me strengthening and encouraging me.

The day arrived when I decided to go to the supermarket for the first time. This would be my first outing since my healing. I parked my car in the car park and walked through the main doors and looked for a trolley. I then noticed that they were all stacked outside . . . staring at me. The annoying voice told me I would never make it.

This scripture came to my mind:

'I can do all things through Christ who strengthens me.'
(Philippians 4:13)

I spoke out God's word and stepped forward. He gave me the strength not only to fetch the trolley, but to fill it up, take all the shopping home, unload and bring it all into the house (I had to climb several steps which led to my front door) put it all away in the appropriate cupboards . . . and still have the energy to make a cup of tea!

To be part of the normal world again was a joy, not only for me but also for my family and friends. The manner in which I returned to health, however, did cause problems with some people. This was a great frustration to me. For years I had been suffering from an incurable illness, trying to convince many that M.E. was indeed a physical disease, and now I was trying to proclaim that I had received divine healing. Accepting scepticism of the reality of M.E. was frustrating. Accepting their unbelief of my miracle I found more upsetting.

Fortunately, my doctor was not in that category. I made an appointment to visit his surgery, something I had not done for a very long time since I always had home visits. As soon as I walked into the surgery, he knew that something had happened to me. He was very interested to hear my story and wrote it down in my medical notes. His comment was one of total acceptance. He shared that he had witnessed this sort of thing before, and believed in the power of prayer.

About twelve months after my healing I went to visit a doctor in Birmingham for a full medical examination for a life insurance policy. I was thinking of going into business with some friends – opening up a Christian tearoom and bookshop in our city. The doctor looked at my very thick medical file, examined me, listened to my story and took notes. He did not say very much, but several days later, I heard that I had been granted the policy. It was for £140,000, and it could be paid at the lowest premium possible! (The Lord actually closed my pursuit of the tearooms, but I believe that in His timing there will be such a place in our city.)

I also became increasingly aware that Jesus could heal me of my thyroid complaint. I had been prescribed the drug Thyroxine, which I was meant to take for the rest of my life, for an under-active thyroid.

I carried a medical exemption card with me, which enabled me to have these drugs free of charge. I made up my mind to stop taking my medication. I knew that for me it was the right thing to do. I had been praying about it for some time and I believe it was the gentle conviction of the Holy Spirit that gave me the peace in my heart. Unless you have divine revelation yourself, it could be very dangerous to stop any medication without medical advice.

Six weeks later, the results of my blood test came back and it was normal. My thyroid was functioning perfectly. The Pathology Department at the local hospital requested a repeat blood test as they could not understand the results. When the second and third test proved to be normal, they too accepted my story. I have never taken any drugs since that time and any subsequent tests have always been normal.

I began to attend St Paul's Church in Worcester and it was good to be part of a church that was hungry for the things of God. I soon made many good friends who encouraged and helped me in my Christian walk. One of the first things I wanted and knew I had to do was to be baptised by full immersion. This was my first step of obedience according to the Scriptures.

> '. . . Repent, and let every one of you be baptised in the name of Jesus Christ for the remission of sins . . . '   (Acts 2:38)

Sunday, 28th October 1990 was the day I was baptised. Sadly, none of my family were able to attend, but many of my friends shared that very special day with me. My baptism signified to me my personal death, burial and resurrection to a new life in Christ.

I began to look forward to actively serving the Lord in some of the work in the church. I was not sure in what form that would take, but God had His way of showing me. One day it was announced that a team of young people would be coming to the church to take a workshop, demonstrating school assembly skills. Host families would be needed, and so I volunteered. On the appropriate day, I went to collect my guest, only to find that I had arrived much too early, and so I was invited to join them. Before I knew what was happening, I was asked if I would like to take part. I was impressed by their professionalism. I was wondering what I was doing this for and was thinking about a recent conversation I had had with a friend who had shared with me about the undisciplined behaviour and difficulties she faced as a teacher in the comprehensive school where she taught. I said to the Lord, 'That school would be a good school for such an assembly!' Little did I know when I prayed that prayer what God had in mind. This is how He brought it all into being.

Shortly after my healing, I went to watch my sons play cricket. I parked my car in a secluded place and hid my handbag under the passenger seat. It was the one and only time I had ever done this, but under the circumstances, I thought it would be quite safe. However, on my return to the car, I discovered that the rear window had been smashed and the bag stolen. It was a shock. The police came and took a statement, telling me that it was extremely unlikely that it would ever be recovered. It would probably have been thrown in the river.

I was very upset, as there were personal things in the bag that I treasured; a poem that Matthew had written when he was thirteen years old and two photographs. To me, these where irreplaceable. After the police had left, I prayed to the Lord. I knew that He could see exactly where the bag was!

I simply asked Him if He would return it to me. I never doubted that my prayer would not be answered. I resisted the temptation to replace both the wallet and purse, and patiently waited.

About four months later, there was a knock at the door of my home. Daniel opened the door to find two policemen standing outside holding my handbag. Apparently it had just been discovered by four schoolboys who had handed it in to their headmaster. He, in turn, had rung the police. As I listened to their story, I examined the bag for the contents. How thrilled I was to find that everything was still there, the poem and the photographs, the only thing missing was a small amount of change and a few 'home help stamps'! Everything was in perfect condition, just as if it had been kept in a top drawer. No sign of dampness or mould. The incredible thing that I discovered later was that the bag had been outside, lying on top of a wall. Ivy had grown over the wall partly camouflaging it and a few spiders had made it their home. During these months, Worcester had suffered severe rainfall and the cricket ground and surrounding areas had been submerged in several feet of water. How could this handbag have been preserved in this condition when it had been exposed to that kind of weather? Only God knew the answer, but one thing was certain, He had heard my prayer.

By this time, both policemen were looking bewildered. I showed them my disabled badge that had been in the bag and shared with them how Jesus had healed me. They could see that it was mine and that I was quite well. They began to realise that there was something very unusual about this case! They then explained to me the usual procedure of recovery of stolen property. The stolen article is taken to the police station, an itinerary taken, the owner notified for identification purposes, then a document is signed and the article returned to the rightful owner. These policemen had never taken anything straight to the owner before.

'I suppose He told you that too!' one of them stated, and looking bewildered but delighted, they both left. It was an amazing testimony to the grace and love of our Father. The next day, I rang the headmaster and asked if I could go into the school to thank the boys personally.

He invited me to go the following lunchtime. I realised that the Lord had given me another opportunity to share the gospel message. I was also aware of the very limited time I would have. I began to be overawed by the situation, but the Lord was so gracious, and showed me exactly what I had to do. Jesus always ministered to the practical needs of the people before He gave them the spiritual food. I wrote the names of each boy on the front of each envelope and placed inside a love gift, and a copy of Matthew's poem. I began to wonder what I would say to them. I wanted to tell them how I had prayed for the return of the handbag, how I had met the Lord and of how He had healed me. I wanted to tell them that Jesus loved them, understood them, knew each one personally and of the importance of asking Him into our lives. I began to panic.

How could I just walk into a school I did not know, meet the master and face these young people and say all I wanted to? It all seemed too much and I began to pray for the Lord to give me strength. I picked up my Bible and turned to the story of Moses. Here was this very humble man, who was asked to do so much by God. I read how inadequate he felt every time he stepped out in faith. But then we read about the wonderful promises of God. For He tells Moses that he will not be alone for God will be with him. He will give him all the strength and courage he will need to fulfil God's work and bring glory to His name.

I knew that God was speaking to me and telling me that as I stepped out in faith He would give me the words to say, just as He had always done. God never changes. His faithfulness is the same today.

I arrived at the school and was taken into the study where I met the deputy headmaster. I explained to him briefly what

I wanted to say to the boys. He was very encouraging and supportive. The boys came into the room and sat opposite me. They explained how they had suddenly spotted the bag lying on top of a wall near to the school. They listened to all that I had to say. I just knew that Lord was with us that lunchtime.

As a direct result of that incident, one of the boys showed the poem to his English teacher who read it out to the class. I asked if it was possible for our newly formed schools' team to take an assembly. This was granted, and when the day arrived, I went to support them, and subsequently, they asked me if I would join the team. We were able to go into this school and many others for several years, taking assemblies and encouraging their Christian Unions. The school was the very same school that I had silently prayed for all those weeks ago. All the years of my theatrical training, plus my former career working with children, was now being used to glorify God. I have come to the conclusion that it does not matter how old you are, when God calls you, He will use all the gifts that He has given to you for His glory.

Thirteen years after this incident, I am still using the very same wallet and purse. Their condition has not deteriorated. Surely signs that make you wonder!

Matthew's poem

My Friend

He has more friends than anyone else in the world,
And yet, only a few have ever met Him.
He taught,
And yet, He was no scholar.
The honest sought redemption from Him,
And yet He gave it to the evil.
The honest offered their homes,
And yet He spent time with sinners.
He is a King,
And yet He has no crown.
He brought a message,
And yet no man would receive it.
He had no palace,
But chose to live the simple life.
He lived amongst men,
And yet man would not accept Him.
He was condemned to death,
And yet He could not hate His persecutors.
He died.
And yet He rose again.
He ascended into heaven,
And yet His memory lives on.
He is supreme Judge.
And yet He is no barrister.
For, Jesus Christ is alone,
The most perfect man.
Although so perfect,
His message is simple,
Love and hope.

Chapter 10

Preparation

'For we are His workmanship,
created in Christ Jesus for good works,
which God prepared beforehand
that we should walk in them.'
(Ephesians 2:10)

I made many friends through St Paul's church who continued to encourage me in my faith. In 1992 I met a wonderful man of God who was affectionately known as Pastor Les. He was already in his late eighties and had served the Lord most of his life as a pastor. He was now an elder of our church. He had a wonderful sense of humour and I loved being in his company. I thought that if I could have chosen a father, it would have been him. I asked him one day if I could look upon him as my adopted spiritual father and he agreed. From that moment onwards I called him Papa Les. I learnt much from him, for example, how to trust God implicitly, to never give up, and to press on with the job in hand. He had a great burden for prayer and taught me much about crying out to God from your heart for the needs of others. I spent many intercessory prayer times with him. He had a particular burden for the people of China. I have no doubt that God had put His seal on our relationship and I truly loved him as a father.

St Paul's Church – 'March for Jesus'

There were many opportunities to learn about the Bible through various seminars and teaching programmes. I enrolled to attend a year's Bible study course headed by our Pastor, Peter Boyd, and Bible teacher, Tony Chamberlain. Many gifted speakers came to talk to us. It was during this time that I was challenged and excited about the prospect of foreign missions. I told the Lord that if He wanted to use me in this way, I would be willing to go 'wherever the need was most'. My prayer was soon answered.

In the spring of 1993, Tony and Pat Chamberlain were planning a three-week trip to the Philippines, taking a party of four people with them. I was to be part of that team. Tony and Pat had for a long time been involved with helping to establish a Bible School in Bacnotan, a small village some eight hours drive from the capital, Manila. We would be going to take part in a crusade at the Bible School and then travel 5,000 feet up into the mountains to Baguio City for a further crusade. I had seen photographs and had heard about the Philippines for some time. I knew that it was a very poor country, extremely hot and humid and would be physically, extremely demanding. I would need to have many injections and take malaria tablets for several weeks, before, during and after my return home. I asked the Lord to confirm to me in every situation if this was His will that I should go. I made an appointment to visit my doctor, who in turn was very encouraging and pleased that I had been given this opportunity. He gave me a perfect opening to share about my experiences when he spoke to the nurse who would be treating me. Picking up the telephone, he said, 'I am sending a patient to you, who has had the worst case of full-blown, chronic M.E. that I have ever seen. She will tell you how she got better!' What an opening! I met such a lovely nurse, who was going through difficulties in her own life, and was so interested in my story. Over the next few weeks, as I went for the various injections, she shared with me that she had prayed that God would help her.

As the time drew nearer for the trip, I began to have moments of sheer panic. I would wake up in the middle of the night and everything would overwhelm me. What if I was ill over there? What if I let down the other members of the team, because I might not be able to keep up with them? I had to be realistic. I could possibly die out there. I would never come home again . . . never see my family. Through all these thoughts, God was asking me if I would really give up every thing for His name's sake. We often say things with our lips, but do we mean it? I knew that I only had one choice. Wherever and whatever God asked of me, I would be obedient.

During these times of seeking God He was so faithful and gave me several promises from the Scriptures on which I could stand. My main concern was for my continued strength and health. One evening, I took Bronwyn for a walk across the beautiful fields at the back of my house. I took my Bible with me as I often find that God speaks to me during these peaceful times. It was a warm summer's evening, and I sat down in the middle of the field, drinking in the beauty of God's creation. The Malvern Hills stretched before me with the woodland behind. We had just had a spell of hot weather. The grass had turned yellow and the wild flowers were beginning to fade. The red sun, hung low in the evening sky and there was a warm, gentle breeze. I could sense the presence of angels around me and I felt the closeness of the Lord. He knew what was on my mind. I was thinking again about my physical strength and the demands this trip would have upon me. I picked up my Bible and my eyes fell on these words:

> 'He gives power to the weak,
> And to those who have no might He increases strength.
> Even the youths shall faint and be weary,
> And the young men shall utterly fall,
> But those who wait upon the LORD
> Shall renew their strength;
> They shall mount up with wings like eagles,
> They shall run and not be weary,
> They shall walk and not faint.'   (Isaiah 40:29–31)

I knew that God was speaking to me personally.

Another scripture the Lord gave me was Psalm 91, and in particular, verses 9–13:

> 'Because you have made the LORD, who is my refuge,
> Even the Most High, your habitation,
> No evil shall befall you,
> Nor shall any plague come near your dwelling;
> For He shall give His angels charge over you,
> To keep you in all your ways.

They shall bear you up in their hands,
Lest you dash your foot against a stone.
You shall tread upon the lion and the cobra,
The young lion and the serpent you shall trample
  underfoot.'

These were promises that I knew had been given to me and when I needed help I knew would be able to remember them and experience the truth and power of His word.

Chapter 11

My First Missionary Trip

'Your word is a lamp to my feet
And a light to my path.'
(Psalm 119:105)

The flight was booked for the 12th October, and it would take approximately nineteen hours to reach Manila. A week before I was due to leave, I developed a sore throat and began to feel unwell. I was not able to sleep and lay awake each night. My doctor prescribed antibiotics. Was God closing the door? Surely He did not intend me to go now? Perhaps He was just testing me, to see if I would be willing to go, as He did with Abraham and Isaac (Genesis 22). I prayed so hard, but I knew that in spite of the circumstances, I had to go. I asked God to give me an understanding of this trial, what was He saying to me? In the early hours of the morning, I read these words:

'Is this not the fast I have chosen:
To loose the bonds of wickedness,
To undo the heavy burdens,
To let the oppressed go free,
And that you break every yoke?
Is it not to share your bread with the hungry,
And that you bring to your house the poor
*   who are cast out;*

When you see him naked, that you cover him,
And not hide yourself from your own flesh?
Then your light shall break forth like morning,
Your healing shall spring forth speedily,
And your righteousness shall go before you;
The glory of the LORD shall be your rear guard.
Then you shall call, and the LORD will answer;
You shall cry, and He will say, "Here I am."'

(Isaiah 58:6–9)

The Lord was clearly telling me that I was going in His strength and not my own. He was reminding me again, that I could do nothing without Him, and that as I stepped out in faith, He would supply all that I needed. How wonderfully He comforted me, and gave me the assurance of His presence at all times.

I spent the rest of the day packing and went to bed feeling very peaceful. Just as I was about to go to sleep, there was a knock at my door and Daniel appeared. He came to my bedside and kneeling down, committed me to the Lord asking Him to look after me and to bring me back safely. There was nothing more to be said.

In the morning Papa Les came to say goodbye to the team. Although there was no opportunity for a private final farewell, as I boarded the bus that was to take us to Heathrow airport, the look on his face told me everything. I knew that he would be praying for me.

We flew from Heathrow to Amsterdam and then onto Manila via Bangkok. We had so much luggage with us, mostly gifts that we were taking to the Filipino people. This included three typewriters and baby equipment for 'Shalom Bata Baby Rescue Centre', which was being run by Ernie and Shirley Fable. The flight was smooth, with the exception of an electrical storm over Bangkok airport that prevented us from landing. We circled round and round over the airport until it passed. This allowed me to see very clearly the impressive views of that city and the surrounding country-side. That sight, plus the vastness of India from air, will never leave me.

We arrived in Manila to be greeted by warm rain. It was just like being in a hot sauna! First impressions, apart from the climate, were the noise of the traffic and the tremendous poverty. Although I had some idea what to expect, it was still a great culture shock to see people living on the pavements in such apparent need. I could see that God had been preparing me all my life for this trip. (As a young woman I first saw real poverty in the Spanish countryside.) I found that I adapted quickly to the oppressive heat and had an instant love for the people. I was fascinated by it all. We arrived at the Christian Mission Centre and were greeted by a smiling Ernie and Shirley Fable. After fellowship, a shower and a cold coke, I went to my bedroom, which I shared with a seventy-nine-year-old lady. She told me that her name was Lou, and she had come over on her own from the west coast of America to minister to the churches. She shared her concern that there was much to do before the Lord returns. I was beginning to realise that as long as you are willing, the Lord will use you at any age!

Both Lou and I were tired and as she had a very early flight the next morning, we said, 'goodnight' to each other and went to sleep. After a few hours, I suddenly woke up. I was facing the wall, but felt as if the Lord was telling me to turn over and face my companion and that I was to pray for her. As I began to pray, suddenly, she sat upright in her bed, got out of it and walked to the door, opened it and looked out. I could see her silhouette clearly, as the landing light had been left on. I thought she was going to the bathroom, but she turned around, shut the door and sat on her bed. She repeated this many times and I wondered what I should do. My first instinct was to speak to her and ask her if she was all right, but I knew that this was the very thing I was not to do. Was she sleepwalking? It was quite frightening to witness this figure dressed in a long white gown behaving oddly in the room. Perhaps I was hallucinating after my long-haul flight! I then remembered His promise to me that:

'No evil shall befall you.'   (Psalm 91:10)

God was showing me His purpose, and I believe that He wanted me to pray for protection for my new friend. She eventually went out of the room, shut the door and was away for about five minutes. I lay in the dark praying in the Spirit until she returned. She repeated the same thing again; only this time staying away for longer, but the Lord gave me a peace about her. When she eventually returned, she climbed back into bed and we both fell asleep!

The next thing I knew, I was being shaken and a voice said to me, 'Gillian wake up! You are late for breakfast.'

It was Pat. I had overslept. I looked at the empty bed next to me. My companion Lou had gone, no doubt safely on board her flight, and homeward bound.

Chapter 12

Falling in Love with
the Philippines

'Get out of your country,
From your kindred ...
To a land that I will show you.'
(Genesis 12:1)

After breakfast, we set off in a small van to the main bus station, where we caught a large air-conditioned bus for our journey to San Fernando. It was fascinating to see the countryside, heartbreaking to see the poverty and distressing to see so many 'cult churches'.

A few hours into our journey, we stopped and had an opportunity to buy refreshments, stretch our legs and go to the loo. I can testify that was an experience I find hard to describe! By this time, the sun was burning down relentlessly, but once we boarded our air-conditioned bus again, the temperature was similar to a summer's day in England. I do thank God that He broke me in gently.

After travelling a few more hours (the whole trip takes between seven and eight hours), there was a smell of rubber. The tyre on the wheel over which I was sitting, burst, and we came to a sudden halt. People noisily got down from the bus to inspect the damage. Buses in the Philippines do not carry spare tyres. (The ones they use anyway look like remoulds of remoulds!). The impression I gathered from the heated debate that was going on outside the bus, was that we would probably be sitting there for the rest of the day. It was obviously quite a common occurrence. We prayed specifically for someone to bring the right tyre, so that we could continue with our journey. The Lord replied very quickly. A passing truck carrying a spare tyre stopped. The tyre was fitted [exactly] and off we started again for our final part of the journey!

On our arrival, we went to meet Pastor Abby at his orphanage. We were greeted by children of all ages who ran and put their arms around us. It was a joy to see so many smiling happy faces. We then boarded another small bus that took us to Andy and Tracy Newlove's home where we would be stopping for a few days.

I had a little room to myself and everything I could possibly need. We gathered together for a meal of rice, a tasty stew and I ate my first 'home grown' banana. It was delicious! The date was 14th October, and Matthew's twenty-second birthday. I was able to use Andy's telephone and call home. Telephones are not readily available in the Philippines, and I saw this again as God's provision for me. Only He knew how important it was for me to be able to speak to my son. I went to bed rejoicing in His goodness.

Pat woke me up at 9 a.m. Late again for breakfast! I had enjoyed a much needed night's sleep, and woke refreshed. After a time of prayer, we went down to the centre of San Fernando to visit the market. We travelled on a jeepney, which is the normal mode of transport in these islands. Jeepneys look as if they are made of shiny tin, very brightly painted and decorated in every colour imaginable. Everyone piles in and sit squashed together on two parallel bench-type seats. When the jeepney is full, the remaining passengers hang from the back, the sides and if necessary, the roof! There is always room for one more on a jeepney. The driver then tears through the traffic with no apparent regard for any highway code. No one has to take a driving test out here, and there is no such thing as an MOT. I thought they were great fun.

It was very hot, humid, noisy and dusty, but I loved the atmosphere. The market was typical, crammed full of stalls with the local people selling anything and everything. After changing some money, I purchased a pair of flip-flops. The Filipinos have small feet like me, so it was great to have a choice! We also bought mosquito nets. The market streets and alleyways were packed with people trading their wares. Shoe cleaners, leather craftsmen, and pots and pans of every description, all waiting to be purchased. Bargaining becomes an art and part of the fun of market shopping. Because we were white, most Filipinos thought we were rich Americans! It was not long before the heat began to take its toll on our yet un-acclimatised bodies, and so we decided to make our way home. Pat and I got into the sidecar of a motorbike, while Mike, a team member, sat behind the motorbike driver, and off we went, trying to avoid the many potholes along the way. These little tricycles make such a noise, almost deafening your ears, and churn up the thick dust as they tear along the roads. That evening, after supper, we gathered for a time of praise and worship before going to bed. However, sleep avoided me, and I finally dropped off at about 5.00 a.m. and woke at 6.45 a.m. I have learned not to become anxious when I have sleepless nights. The Lord knows what we have to get through the next day, and He always gives me the strength to do just that. I often stand on His promise of

'... *As your days, so shall your strength be.*'
(Deuteronomy 33:25)

Later on that day, we travelled to Bacnotan to visit Crossroads Bible Institute. Evening comes quickly in this part of the world and darkness began to fall as we started on our journey. How beautiful to see the huge, orange sun, hovering over the sea's horizon, silhouetting the graceful palm trees before disappearing, turning the red sky, black. What a welcome waited for us as we arrived at the college. Smiling faces and open arms. I was overwhelmed by the love and openly cried. I thanked God that He had allowed me to see for myself, the very place that I had held dear in my heart and prayers.

I was taken to my room, which had a small wooden bed, a chair and an electric fan, of which I was very grateful! There was no mattress on the bed, so I placed several towels on the hard wood base, erected my mosquito net and lit my little burner. We had our evening meal and then it was time for a service of thanksgiving. How the Filipinos love to praise the Lord! After prayers, Tony introduced us to the assembly, and then preached on 'signs and wonders'. By this time, the mosquitoes had come out in full force. I could see thousands of them flying around as they were attracted to the electric light bulb that hung from the ceiling. There were also huge beetles, 3 inches long by 2 inches wide, flying around above our heads and then, dropping like bombers onto the floor only to scurry quickly away. These were definitely not the sort to crush under your feet! The heat was still intense and I was grateful for my hand fan.

After Tony had finished preaching, the people came forward for prayer. I stood and prayed along side them, not knowing their language but having the all-embracing language of the Holy Spirit. The Lord stood in our midst and ministered to us all. We all went to bed, richer people. I was overwhelmed by His love.

The next morning I rose early and had my first shower of the day – using a bucket containing cold water, a ladle and a hole in the floor! We held our morning session of bringing the Word. I was very aware of God's presence not only in the meetings, but also in a personal way. As I began to lean on Him, I began to walk in a completely new freedom.

I ceased to be concerned about drinking the water, wondering whether it had been boiled. I just prayed quietly to Him and I knew in my heart that I could trust Him to look after me.

At lunchtime, we had fellowship with the pastors, who shared with us the political and economic situation in the Philippines. After a rest on my little bed, and another shower, I wandered outside onto the veranda. We overlooked the rice fields and I was fascinated to see the men and women at work. They were gathering the rice crop, in a very primitive way, most of the threshing still being done by hand. It is a common sight to see the rice placed on sacking or polythene sheets and left on the side of the road to dry in the heat. Rice is the staple diet of the Filipinos, but it is quite delicious, so different from the rice we cook in the West! As I returned to my little room, I had a sudden pang of dreadful homesickness. After a little weep, the Lord met my need and I was able to join the other members of the team for another night's ministry.

The following day, it was decided that I would give my testimony at the evening service celebration. I felt very nervous.

After the morning seminar, we caught a jeepney and visited Benguet City (it was not a city in the sense that we understand, in fact it was quite a small village). What a place! It was dusty, noisy and very dirty. We visited the local market, but I am glad to say that we did not buy anything. The smell was overpowering as we walked past tables of raw meat, half-cooked by the heat, and covered by large, black flies that plagued everywhere. Dogs and children were lying together in the dirt. We caught another jeepney that took us to San Fernando, where we bought the things we wanted before we returned home again to the Bible Institute.

I went to my little room, to rest and seek the Lord before the evening service. The sun was beating down on the tin roof, and because of an electricity cut, I was unable to benefit from any relief that the fan could have provided. It is very common not to have electricity during the daytime in the Philippines, especially in the more remote areas. Pat joined me for prayer and encouragement. As we prayed, we had the impression that there were angels surrounding the Bible College. We knew that the Lord was going to move on the hearts of His people. Becky Tamaken, daughter of the Pastor, ministered in song. It was a very special time for us all. I then got up to share my experiences. I had a lovely interpreter who stood next to me. The Holy Spirit helped me to recall all that was needed and I knew that He was setting captives free and healing people. It was again, humbling to think that I who had been called by the grace of God, saved, healed and delivered and was now able to stand before these beautiful people and share His love. After I had finished speaking, Pastor Tamaken prayed and suddenly a sea of faces stood before us, weeping and crying out to the Lord. Everyone had left their seats and come forward to receive prayer. Young people gave their lives to the Lord, others were ministered to in their deepest needs as Jesus touched them. Some were set free from demons and filled with God's love.

It was an evening that I shall never forget.

Chapter 13

Falling in Love with the Filipinos

'Beloved, let us love one another,
for love is of God ... '
(1 John 4:7)

The next morning, as I went to take my shower, a sharp pain suddenly gripped me. I felt very sick and faint and tried to get back to my bed. I began to pray in tongues. In my spirit, I knew that I was under attack and that I needed the prayers of my friends. I slowly made my way down to the kitchen, where I found Pastor Tamaken's wife, Rebecca. She sat me in a chair and called for her daughters to come and pray for me. They all laid hands on me and prayed against the attack and for God's protection. Within a few minutes, the pain had completely gone and I was able to continue with my plan of visiting Pastor Abby's orphanage.

When I arrived at the orphanage, a crowd of smiling, brown faces greeted me. The children, who had been expecting me, excitedly led me to their classroom. The room was very basic compared to our standards with just a few wooden benches and bare concrete walls. They sang some lovely songs to me, and in return I was able to teach them some of the choruses and songs that we sing in England. We then began to work on a frieze of Noah's Ark, which the older children mounted and placed on the walls. When it was completed, it looked very effective. Soon, it was time for me to return to the Bible College, and so I said my goodbyes and told them that I would be returning the following morning.

It was wonderful how the Lord had placed on my heart, exactly what I should bring with me when I left England. There had been no definite plans for me to work with children, and yet I felt the Lord had told me exactly how many pieces of paper, coloured card, books, pencils and crayons to take. On my return the next day, we spoke about creation, and working in groups, completed the story using all the available materials. Once mounted, the appropriate text was written at the base of each picture. How effective it all looked. It was a precious time that I spent with the children, and again, an experience that I shall never forget. All these children had heartbreaking stories to tell, and yet seemed so happy and content. Truly, witnesses of the contentment that there is to be found in knowing the Lord Jesus. We have much to learn from them. All too soon it was time for me to say goodbye.

When I arrived back at CBI (Crossroads Bible Institute) I had a late lunch and then went to my room, where I slept for an hour. I was beginning to experience some sound sleep, in spite of the heat and lack of mattress! The Filipino girls work so hard, constantly washing and ironing their few clothes in order to keep themselves clean and fresh. They would sit with buckets of cold water and bars of soap, no washing machines for them to use. Most of them are up each morning at 5.00 a.m. By the time I went down to get my breakfast each morning, their lines of washing were nearly dry! I thank the Lord, for the way they undertook for me, insisting on doing all my washing and ironing, and giving up their bed for me – most of these girls slept on just a blanket on the floor. It was lovely to be part of their lives and to live alongside of them, all with the same goal, serving the Lord Jesus Christ.

At the evening meeting, there was again a mighty move of the Holy Spirit and many people came forward for prayer, especially for the baptism in the Holy Spirit.

As we began to pray for them, tiredness swept over me and I felt so ordinary and unworthy to be praying for them. I stood at the back, asking God to forgive me for the way I was feeling. I decided that the best thing was for me to sit down, but just as I was going to, a young girl came up to me and asked me to pray for her. As I began to pray in my exhaustion and weakness, words began to pour from my mouth and I knew that the Lord was ministering to her. What a loving Father we serve, only He knew how much I needed encouragement. He was showing me that He uses us as vessels, that it is His power, not ours. Our feelings have nothing to do with the power of God. He touched both the young girl and me that night. The Lord giving her a scripture and meeting her deepest needs in a way that only He knew how. So many people were set free and filled with God's love, and I just stood there and watched it happen.

As the Lord told His disciples in Luke 10:23–24:

> *'. . . Blessed are the eyes which see the things you see; for I tell you that many prophets and kings have desired to see what you see, and have not seen it, to hear what you hear, and have not heard it.'*

Thank you for the privilege Lord.

The next morning I woke early and had my shower (I was still not used to the cold water even in that heat, but it was one way of waking yourself up!). After breakfast, we went down for another morning seminar of teaching. I felt waves of exhaustion sweep over me again, and so Pat advised me to go back to bed, which I gladly did. I awoke, feeling greatly refreshed after a further hour of deep sleep. I was then taken to the top of the complex, where there is an area of concrete laid under a bamboo roof. Because it is fairly high up and has open sides, there was a pleasant breeze. I was able to sit on the wooden bench and rest.

The view was lovely, with rice fields stretching in front of me and again, I could see the workers arriving with their buffalo, called caribao, to begin the day's work. The people wore little Chinese style hats to protect them from the relentless sun. I could hear them cutting the rice by hand and then thrashing the grain. The work was slow and hard. The dogs played beneath me on the ground with their puppies, and the chickens scratched for food in the dust. I could see more chickens in bamboo cages not far from me, and three large pigs lay in a concrete pen. It was good to drink in the atmosphere and also try and put names to the many new faces that I had met. Some of the young pastors came and spoke to me, and although I could not understand their dialect, they had a good understanding of English.

That evening, Pat and I were asked to do a drama. We had done one the previous evening that seemed to have been gratefully appreciated. The meeting started at 6.45 p.m. with praise and worship, and then each person was invited to give their testimony. I noticed the little girl I had prayed with the night before, looking radiant as she shared God's grace. I did not understand a word of what she was saying, but just to see the change in her was enough.

Bob Lillyman, one of the team members and a very gifted Bible teacher, gave his testimony of how God had kept him during his years of active service in the police force. He began to explain to us his experience of God's protection. He was part of a 2,000 contingent of policemen who had gathered together, to control a dangerous demonstration from thousands of people in the streets.

These were armed rioters, bent on destruction and particularly aggressive towards the police. Bob was part of a line of men, linked arm to arm, stretching across the road to stop the oncoming mass of rioters marching towards them. It was a very dangerous and nerve-racking situation as they could only stand to form a human wall to the oncoming demonstrators. When the vast crowd of rioters came to within six feet of the police, they stopped, stared and then calmly turned around and retreated to where they had come from! Bob was to discover later, that at that precise moment, his mother had been in a prayer meeting, when a woman stopped the prayer time and said that they were to start praying for Bob because he was in danger! That is the power of prayer.

A baptismal service had been arranged for the new converts, and this was to take place at a nearby waterfall. We piled into our jeepney that took us as far as it could go, and then we covered the rest of the ground on foot. What a spectacular place it was! We made our way over high boulders that rose above the rushing waters. It was so peaceful and I could hear clearly the sounds of the different birds. I saw beautiful butterflies, bright yellows, blues, and some species with huge black and white wings. The narrow river bed ran between high cliffs that stretched many feet above us on either side. Tropical vegetation grew up these sheer cliffs and huge trees looked down on us from the top. When we eventually reached the waterfall, what a sight met our eyes. Crystal clear waters cascading down into a deep pool below, sending out a continuous spray of tiny droplets of cold water like a fine mist, which sprayed us as we drew closer. Looking back down the ravine, I could begin to imagine a little of how the Garden of Eden must have looked. It was a very moving time, especially for the young men who were being baptised. We held a service of prayer, and sang as they came out of the waters. When it was over, we made our way back over the streams and rocks. It was early afternoon and the hot sun was beginning to take its effect on me. It had yet again been a full day, demanding both on my physical strength and stamina. As I walked down from the waterfall, Tony told me to look up and there flying majestically above us, soaring and hovering in the sky was the most beautiful eagle with his wings stretched out. What a sight! I remembered the promise that God had given me back home, as I sat in my field:

> *'But those who wait on the LORD*
> *Shall renew their strength;*
> *They shall mount up with wings like eagles,*
> *They shall run and not be weary,*
> *They shall walk and not faint.'* (Isaiah 40:31)

Yes! I was walking in the oppressive heat, and I was strong and not faint. How precious are His promises and how faithful is our Lord.

After returning to CBI, we packed our bags and set off on the second part of our mission, which would be held in Baguio City, 5,000 feet up in the mountains.

Chapter 14

Beautiful Baguio

'He has put a new song in my mouth –
Praise to our God.'
(Psalm 40:3)

We all piled into Andy Newlove's air-conditioned pick-up truck and set off on our journey. It was so comfortable after the jeepneys, and much appreciated for the journey ahead. For the next two hours, we climbed 5,000 feet up into the mountains. The views were breathtaking. Lush vegetation was blooming profusely after the rainy season. Huge red poinsettias, with flower heads the size of dinner plates, were growing wildly, forming high hedges. It was not long before we were above the clouds! The roads were absolutely appalling; just very narrow dirt tracks with huge potholes. There were places where parts of the road had literally fallen away down the mountainside. A recent typhoon had caused more damage, and we could see groups of workmen trying to mend the roads. It was pathetic to witness them trying to do their best with such primitive tools, and under such difficult conditions. Much poverty again was very evident, as we passed tiny tin and bamboo shacks where families huddled together.

As we climbed nearer to the top of the mountains, we could see Baguio city in front of us. What a surprise! It was so different from my expectations. Hundreds of little houses seem to cling to the sides of the hills, as if they had been stuck there with blu-tac! On entering the city, I was aware of the wealth and poverty existing side by side. The Americans built this city during the Second World War and much of their influence was still evident.

Narrow busy streets, packed with Filipino people who looked so different from the Filipinos we had just left in San Fernando. There are so many different tribes of people who inhabit these many islands, and each speaks a different dialect. Eventually, we arrived at the Missionary Centre, which would be our base for the next five days. What another surprise in store for us! It was like walking into another world. As I entered the building, I could see that it was built of highly polished wood, ceiling to floor. The rooms were huge, all with comfortable chairs, just waiting to be sat in! My room had a double bed with a very deep mattress, a writing table, chair, footstool, and table lamp, separate dressing room and opposite my room a real bathroom with shower and running hot and cold water. How grateful I was for the Lord's abundant provision. Only He knew how tired I was just beginning to feel, and now He had provided me with all this luxury.

After a supper of beefburgers, lettuce, tomatoes, bread and butter, jelly and de-caffeinated coffee, and a quick glance of the news on the television, our first contact with the outside world for ten days, I crept into bed.

The following morning, I was greeted with an English breakfast, but as delicious as it looked, I found that I could only eat a small amount. My stomach had adjusted to the rice diet and I found the food very rich. We decided to explore Baguio market, which had the reputation of being one of the best markets in the world. Again, it was a wonderful experience to wander through the narrow alleyways, packed with hundreds of stalls, everyone selling their wares. The weather is so much cooler up here, similar to a hot summer day in England. and it made a refreshing change. The Filipinos however, were wearing woollen jumpers and hats!

The food market had an abundance of various fruit and vegetables. It all looked very clean and fresh, and most notable was the absence of flies. It seemed a world away from the market at Benguet. As I walked up the street, I noticed a blind man sitting on the dusty pavement. He held a small bowl in his hand that contained a few coins. I knew that the Lord was giving me an opportunity to speak of His love. I knelt beside him, and told him about the love of Jesus. I was amazed by how much English he seemed to understand. I hope he understood a little of what I was saying, but as I left, he smiled. It was not long before I realised that there were many like him, begging men, women and children were a common sight. A little old woman, bent double, approached me and leaning heavily on her walking stick put out her wrinkled brown hand. A policeman came over and warned me not to get involved with these 'professional' beggars. I wonder what Jesus would have done?

As we continued to mingle with the crowd, suddenly a woman came up to Pat and pointed to her handbag. It had been slashed with a knife and her purse had been stolen. Crime is rife here and foreigners are vulnerable, so we took extra care to protect ourselves. On returning to our base, we had a tasty lunch, and then I went to my room to spend time in preparation for the next day's ministry. It had been decided that each of us would go to a different church and bring a message. I was to go with sister Becky Tamaken, who would be my interpreter, to a church in Slide Tuding. I felt the Lord had nudged me to speak on the trials of Joseph and of how through this preparation, God had been able to use him in a mighty way (Genesis 37–50). I would also share my testimony of healing. It was to be a demanding time, but I knew that He would help and guide me.

I rose at 6.30 a.m. the following morning in order to catch the jeepney for the journey ahead. It was interesting to see another part of Baguio. There seemed to be so many young people here, and I soon discovered that out of the population of 300,000, two-thirds of that number is made up of students. There are in fact five universities in this city. It was not long before we were back onto the muddy tracks of the narrow road, with sheer drops falling hundreds of feet into the valleys below. Once again the scenery was spectacular with enormous green mountains and sudden deep valleys, all at different levels. The roads were either very steep or sloped dangerously downwards. At one point, we had to do a three-point turn on a very narrow strip of road. As the driver manoeuvred the jeepney, the rear wheels seemed to hang very close to the precipice. I drew comfort from the fact that the Lord said He would be our rear guard! As the jeepney straightened around to face the right way, I sighed with relief! The morning had only just begun.

Eventually, the jeepney stopped at our destination, and sister Becky and I got out. We made our way down a narrow rough track that dropped down the side of the steep hill. At one time, the long grass was up to my waist, making my clothes wet from the morning dew. It was difficult to see where we were going. I remembered that snakes are common in the Philippines, and I prayed that the Lord would spare me of such an encounter! We arrived at the little church, which was just a bamboo hut with a tin roof. There were a few wooden benches inside, a blackboard and a stand for the Bible. The floor was the earth, and one of the sides was completely open. The view was breathtaking, stretching across and over the mountains and valleys with lush vegetation as far as the eye could see. It was 8.00 a.m. and no one had yet arrived. Becky took me further down the track that dropped deeper into the valley, until we arrived at the pastor's house. What a lovely little haven it was. So simple, yet set in a peaceful quiet garden.

I sat on a wooden bench and watched the family pig as he grunted in his bamboo cage. The family, who again had a good comprehension of English, greeted me warmly.

At 9.00 a.m, we climbed back up the hill to the church to begin our morning service. What a joyful time it was, all praising the Lord for His goodness, old and young alike, united in His love. The Holy Spirit was with us, as sister Becky ministered in song, and as I brought the message. As I stood there, it was as if everything came flooding back into my mind. The memory of all the years of pain and the hopelessness and despair of being 'trapped' in a sick body. I had to pinch myself to see if it was real. For a moment, I thought perhaps it was all a dream and I would wake up to find myself back in bed! Had it all really happened? Was it really possible for me to be standing here, thousands of miles from home, fit and healthy? The simple truth is, that through Jesus Christ, all things are possible.

> *'Jesus Christ is the same yesterday, today, and forever.'*
> (Hebrews 13:8)

He took our sins and sickness on His body nearly 2,000 years ago. It began and ended at the cross at Calvary. There is no disease or problem that He cannot cure. I, like many others, am a living testimony to His Divine healing. Jesus is Lord, and the world needs to know.

Several days later, my feet stood once again on English soil. I had been changed for life. I knew that I would never be the same again. It was wonderful to be home and to see my family, but I found it difficult to settle. Reverse culture shock on my return was also something that I had not accounted

Once again on English soil . . . [left to right] *Daniel, me, Matthew*

for. It took me many days to adjust to the rich diet and the abundance of wealth that we have at out fingertips.

I knew that it was only a matter of time before I would return.

Chapter 15

My Second Missionary Trip

' "You know that I love You." ...
Jesus said to him, "Feed My sheep." '
(John 21:16, 17)

My yearning to return to the Philippines became part of my life, and yet I had to be quite sure it was a desire that the Lord had placed in my heart and not one of my own ambitions. He confirmed to me, that a door would be opened and I would know when. Several months passed and then I received an invitation from Pastor Tamaken asking me if I would return to the Bible Institute to teach the students English. When I read the letter, I cried, for I knew that this was what the Lord was asking me to do. I shared with my Pastor, who felt it was God's will, and that I should be prepared to go out for several months.

I talked in great depth with Papa Les. At first he was quite alarmed and told me he did not want me to go. His health had been causing him problems and he had been diagnosed as suffering from cancer. It was a great blow and leaving him would be far greater now that perhaps his time on earth was limited. I think he finally recognised God's calling on my life and gave me his blessing. He supported me both prayerfully and financially.

My family were naturally concerned for me, but any worries they may have had, they kept them to themselves.

They demonstrated their love by not forcing their personal feelings onto me. Parting from each other was a two-fold sacrifice.

I committed every detail to the Lord for His undertaking, and He met my needs in every aspect. The finances were met for my airfare, my support whilst abroad, and my own private use. I attended a TEFL course (Teaching English as a Foreign Language) as I felt inexperienced in teaching young people. It was very helpful and again the Lord provided the exact money to finance this, as I had no spare money of my own.

On the 4th October 1994, I flew back out to Manila, via Amsterdam and Bangkok. It was a very different experience from the previous trip in every way. The hardest thing again, was for me to leave behind my loved ones and to step into the unknown. But what joy there is in obedience and what blessings the Lord has for you. I have discovered the two keys to the fulfilment of His plan: to trust and obey.

The heat of Manila hit me once again as I left the aircraft. Why did I find this hot, humid, noisy and dirty place so attractive? Ernie and Shirley Fable met me at the airport. It had been arranged that I would spend two weeks with them, helping to care for the babies and small children. Within a few days I had phased into their hectic routine and it was not long before they also claimed a part of my heart. Many of these little ones had been abandoned, often rescued from certain death, and brought to the home by the Philippine Social Services. Many of them suffered with poor health. Most of them had scabies, dreadful boils, chest infections, TB and parasites. I had much to thank God for. It was only by His love and grace, and the emotional and physical strength He gave, that I was able to help in any effective way. Through many demanding days, and in spite of my failings, God did a great work.

My first crisis occurred twelve days after my arrival. I woke early one morning with an acute pain in my stomach, which made me vomit. I recognised the symptoms as an attack of 'Crohns'. The very thing that I had always dreaded happening, was taking place. I knew the seriousness of it all, and so I shared with Ernie and Shirley, who decided that I needed to be taken to hospital without delay. We drove to Makati hospital, walked in and asked to see a doctor. A specialist, who had been treating Shirley, just happened to be there and had just had a cancelled appointment. I was taken into his surgery straight away. Upon examination, he admitted me to one of the wards, and personally put me on a drip. In spite of the circumstances, I knew that God was in control. I saw that this excellent provision of medical care that was available to me in my hour of need was His way of comforting me. Shirley, who was very tired and suffering from an acute chest infection, stayed with me. It is law in the Philippines that either a relative or friend has to stay and look after the patient if they are admitted to hospital. We spent three days resting and sleeping. What was God saying to me at this time? I believe that when God does not remove painful situations, it is because He is moulding us through them. Jesus brought me through this difficulty, teaching me to totally trust in Him in all circumstances. Every trial can be a place of blessing. God always proves Himself to be a mighty Deliverer. He never fails to plan the best things for us.

A few days after our discharge from hospital, a typhoon struck Manila reaping destruction and leaving us without water or electricity and then. As if this was not enough to contend with, we had another emergency! One of the babies became very ill, and we knew that she would have to be taken to the local hospital without delay. Sick babies can deteriorate and die very quickly, so prompt action often saves their lives. One of the immediate problems we faced was that during the typhoon, a large coconut tree had fallen, blocking the driveway, which made it impossible for us to

José, Rommel and Elvin
holding coconuts blown down during the typhoon

get to the baby ambulance. We all started praying and calling out to God to help us in this seemingly impossible situation. He intervened in a most beautiful way.

From nowhere, four Filipino men appeared, cut up the tree, cleared the driveway, and within twenty minutes, we were on our way to the hospital. On arriving at a Paranaque Hospital, Ernie returned to help Shirley, and I was literally left holding the baby! When I entered the hospital, I felt as if I had stepped back a century in time. It was obviously poorly equipped, shabby and dirty. Only two candles were burning in the whole unit. Two or three patients shared one bed, and each bed was placed closely by one another. I held Marchella, as a tiny intravenous drip was placed in her arm. I was then taken to a bed where I could lay her down. We

Baby Marchella having revcovered from her ordeal at Paranaque hospital and Rommel on his bike. He had been abandoned at birth, blind and retarded, but is now making excellent progress.

shared this with another baby, the baby's mother and grandmother!

In the middle of the ward, lying on a table was a young boy. He had extensive wound injuries and the doctor was stitching his face and head. Several nurses were holding him down. I shall never forget his cries. Six hours later, Marchella had greatly improved and she was allowed to come home.

Several days later, I again accompanied Shirley to the local doctor with three of the babies who needed medication. I carried eighteen-month-old Mark, who was blind. His sight was operable, but his mother refused to have it done because she wanted to use him on the streets. Blind children have more begging appeal.

I believe the Lord brings all these babies here and that He has a plan and a purpose for each of their lives. It was not easy for me to say goodbye to my new family, but I had already been in Manila for a month, and I knew that it was time for me to go to San Fernando, and to Crossroads Bible Institute.

Chapter 16

Learning to Trust in the Lord

'Trust in the LORD with all your heart,
And lean not on your own understanding.'
(Proverbs 3:5)

Ernie had decided to travel with me on the eight-hour coach journey, to help me with my heavy case and to keep me company. I was very grateful to both Ernie and Shirley for their sacrificial giving. After our long, hot journey and a quick cup of tea, Ernie took the next coach back and returned to Manila. Andy Newlove drove me to the Bible Institute, where I was taken to my new room. Life would certainly be very different for the second part of my mission.

Everyone made me feel very welcome, and I had a huge pile of letters waiting for me from home. What joy to ponder over the pages of news. There is a real ministry in writing to people, especially when they are on the mission field. I will always be grateful to everyone who took the time and trouble to write to me. Some letters were from people I hardly knew.

I quickly settled in my room, unpacking my books and personal belongings. I had a foam mattress on my wooden bed, a table and a chair. I erected my mosquito net and was given a fan. It was good to be able to be part of the Bible college, although I was a little dismayed when I discovered that my first lesson was to be the following morning at 8.30 a.m! I was also expected to take Child Psychology lessons twice a week, plus children's Sunday school.

I had a good night's sleep and was woken by the students' early morning praise and worship service (5.00 a.m.). It was lovely to meet all the students and I knew that I would soon have a special relationship with them. They really have a good command of the English language, but eager to learn the skills of grammar and writing techniques. I was anxious about how I should approach the psychology lessons, especially as I had not brought any reference books with me. I came before my Father and asked Him to show me. As I waited on Him, using only the Bible, He gave me twelve full lessons on the subject. I learnt a great deal and believe I understand more, the frailty of a young life and the enormous responsibility of bringing up children correctly. God has given His Word in the Bible, and that is the manual we should draw from if they are to have a good foundation in life. I realised how much I had let my own children down through my own selfishness and ignorance.

The following morning, Becky and her sister Rebecca came with me to the market. We caught a jeepney to the nearest town, a ride of approximately forty-five minutes. As usual, the jeepney was packed, but it was lovely to feel the breeze on my face as we sped along the roads (I had to hold a handkerchief across my mouth to stop breathing in the dust). The countryside is wonderful, varied and fascinating. Rice fields, banana crops, farmers working in their fields with their placid carabaos, little children playing on the side of the roads with just a few sticks, and then suddenly a glimpse of beautiful blue sea! We are on the coast here and although the beaches are perhaps not the most hygienic, the sight, smell and sound of the sea, thrilled me.

Browsing amongst the market traders, we managed to purchase an electric ring for cooking, a few pots and pans and some lovely cane furniture. (This is very cheap to buy in the Philippines.)

I later met Andy and Tracy Newlove, who managed to put me in contact with an American missionary who wanted to sell his refrigerator. I was able to buy this and it was later installed in my room back at CBI. I was well pleased with all these provisions and my room became a palace to me.

Theresa travelled from Baguio to see me; she was an ex-student from the college and a special friend from my previous visit. It was lovely to catch up with all the news. I was quite overwhelmed by all the kindness shown to me, but I still had waves of homesickness. England seemed so far away and I had no means of communication other than post, which sometimes took many days to reach its destination. I now began to cook and look after myself, which had its good and bad points. Being the only English person on the complex, even although I could not have had more caring companions, brought its own frustrations. During devotions that evening, the Lord gave me a picture.

I was standing in the Philippines with my body facing England. The Lord showed me that if I turned round (my back now toward England) I would be able to look at Him full in the face. As I looked at Him with His arms stretched out towards me, I could see that He was not only watching over me, but over all my loved ones at home. He was asking me to trust my family with Him. He alone was sufficient. I felt a new outpouring of His love and I was able to release everything to Him. I asked Him to forgive me and from that moment on I never looked back again. I was able to put my hand to the plough and get on with the job that I was called to do.

I must admit that one of the things I missed the most on coming to Bacnotan, was the children. I asked God that if there perhaps was one child at the Bible school that needed extra love, that He would bring that child to me. It was not

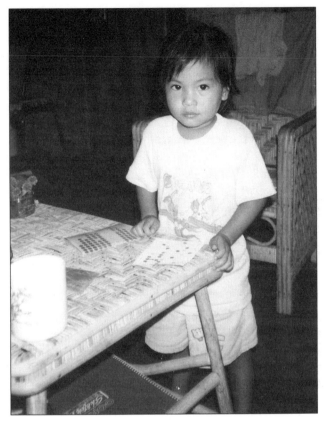

Cathy – my little friend!

long after I had prayed that prayer, that I felt a small brown hand slip into mine and found a large pair of black eyes looking up at me. Cathy and I had a special relationship from that moment on. She would often come for a cuddle and spend time with me in my room, where we would draw pictures and play games. She did not understand any English, but we were able to communicate love.

My time at the orphanage also stood me in good stead when Caleb, the eighteen-month-old son of one of the pastors, became ill. I had heard him crying most of the night and was told that he had a very high fever. I went to see if I could help and found his mother holding him anxiously in her arms. It was obvious from his flushed complexion, that indeed he had a high temperature. The most important thing now, was to do everything possible to bring that down. I had been used to bathing the small babies and children at 'Shalom Bata Rescue Centre' in tepid water, placing fans near to them to try and cool the air. Naturally the little ones protested, but inevitably it worked. Blessing, Caleb's mother, had him wrapped in layers of warm clothing, a woollen hat and knitted booties. It was obvious that she believed that to keep him warm was the right treatment. I had to persuade her otherwise, and ask her to trust me when in fact I wanted her to do the opposite and cool him down. I asked the Lord to give me His wisdom and love for the situation.

Blessing allowed me to take her son, undress him, place him in a cool bathtub and practically drown him in water! At least that is how it sounded as Caleb protested, but within an hour, his temperature had fallen. Needless to say, my relationship with Caleb was now treated with severe caution. From that moment on he would try to avoid me or hide from me whenever we met, just in case I had another cold bath waiting for him!

As I began to adjust to my lifestyle, I found that with the Lord's help, I could take most things in my stride. As I learnt to lean on Him, it once again brought me into a new freedom. I ceased to be concerned about the approaching lessons, as the Holy Spirit directed me for each step of the way. I do not know about the students, but certainly I learnt a great deal.

However, there was an area that I did find difficult on several occasions. I used to lie in bed at night and watch the lizards scrambling across my walls and ceiling, wondering if they would drop onto my net. Would they bounce off, or simply crawl under? I had become accustomed to the mosquitoes and beetles, but was not very happy when I found I shared my loo with a huge spider. His body was as big as my hand, with long hairy legs that were attached to it!

One day, just as dusk was falling, I just 'happened' to look on the floor and saw a scorpion an inch away from my bare foot. I quickly squashed it with a broom, but it was not until later that I realised the potential seriousness of the situation. Andy Newlove in fact told me that he had heard of several people dying from scorpion stings in recent months. I thank God for His protection and promise that 'no deadly thing will harm you' (Psalm 91:10–13) and for the authority that He had given that I was able to *'trample on serpents and scorpions . . . and nothing shall by any means hurt you'* (Luke 10:19).

I was beginning to become very fond of the students, although there was a slight distance between us, probably because I was their 'teacher'. As the weeks went by, one of the students came to my room to share a problem that she had. She was prompted to come and talk with me as a direct result of a recent study we had done on 'Blessings and Curses' through our families. She had always had difficulty when it was her turn to preach the Word. She would become agitated and nervous and not be able to deliver her message. As she shared, and as directed by the Holy Spirit, she was set free from demonic curses and spirits that had oppressed her all her life. Her mother had 'passed her through the waters' to become a medium and spiritualist when she was a baby. She had actually been dedicated to become an agent of Satan. She was totally set free through the power of the blood of Jesus. It was a joy to witness the difference in her face, and she was able to preach her next sermon with boldness.

There were several times when we all gathered together to pray against the attack of the enemy. We had to learn to be discerning, and to take authority as soon as a problem arose. Where God is doing a work, the enemy will do his best to destroy or discourage those involved. We can rejoice that we have the victory in the name of Jesus!

It was time for my weekly visit to San Fernando. I must say I looked forward to going, not only because I knew I would be collecting my post and therefore news from home, but I enjoyed the adventure of the travel. Each week, I took a different student with me. It was good to have their company and have them each in turn. I would take whoever was with me to the Danish pastry café in the town. It was wonderful to go there. Such a selection of delicious cakes and I know that for many of them it was the first time experience of such luxury. We caught the jeepney and then a tricycle to the post office. I would take the key and unlock the box. There was always a pile of letters waiting there!

I would place them into my bag, just feeling them and knowing how I would enjoy opening them, one by one, and savour every word when I returned to my room at Bacnotan.

I would often call at Andy and Tracy Newlove's home to catch up with all their news. It was always good to have fellowship with them and they encouraged and prayed for me.

I was beginning to feel the effects of the climate. I could not stay in my room after 10.00 a.m. as the relentless sun, beating down on the corrugated tin roof, made my room unbearably hot. I would try to seek some respite in the shade, but it was not always possible. You certainly have to take life at a quieter pace. I have noticed that even the birds seem to fly slower out there!

I longed for the fresh breezes of Baguio city. The Lord fulfilled that desire, by sending Theresa to me, who in turn invited me to stay with her and her family for a long weekend. I was feeling very tired and I had noticed that the deafness and ear pain that I had been suffering from for several weeks, was becoming more acute. I packed my bag and waited for her to arrive.

Chapter 17

Hard Work, Rest
and News from Home

'He has made everything beautiful in its time.'
(Ecclesiastes 3:11)

We had a good journey to Baguio, and once again I enjoyed the spectacular scenery. We sat together on a small narrow seat next to the bus driver. Bags of rice were piled in the alley ways and people sat where they could. Again, I held my breath as the driver manoeuvred the bus around the narrow bends. I could see the road through a gaping hole in the floor next to the gear stick!

A few hours later, I was resting on Theresa's bed. In fact I did not get much sleep that night and although I felt physically exhausted, I felt spiritually uplifted. I knew that the Lord had undertaken for me. I spent the next day just chatting to Betty, Theresa's sister, who made me feel so welcome, and resting in my lovely room. The view from the window was breath taking, the mountainous hills stretching before me, and the cool breezes blowing through my window. What a perfect place to rest, and prepare for my schoolwork.

The next day, I was asked if I would speak at a little church in Happy Hollow, a small village down in the nearby valley. The church had been established for six years, so we would

have a celebration service, followed by a meal. I felt the Lord
had given me a word of encouragement for them, to go forth
and evangelise and each member to win one soul for Christ.

We set off at 8.00 a.m. for the walk down the mountains to
Happy Hollow. The road was very steep, and it did cross my
mind as I climbed down that I was going to have to come
back up the same way! Trusting the Lord to give you the
strength certainly gives you a peace that you could not get
from anywhere else! As I continued on my journey, I
remembered the scripture:

> *'He makes my feet like the feet of a deer,*
> *And sets me on my high places.'*   (Psalm 18:33)

The little church was very much like the one I had visited
at Slide Tuding the previous year, with open sides, bamboo
poles and a tin roof. We all gathered together and had a
wonderful time of praise and worship, led by Theresa. One
lady shared her testimony of how God had kept her through
very difficult circumstances (she was married to an unbeliev-
ing husband, who was continually drunk and she had to go
and find food for her children). After the service, we shared
our lunch together of rice, chicken stew and vegetables. I
then rested in a little wooden house before the ascent up the
hills to Theresa's home. The sun was very hot and everyone
found a place to lie down and rest, before making his or her
journey home. When we did finally walk back up the roads, I
was surprised how quickly I found myself at the top, only
having to rest a few times on the way. Needless to say, the
muscles in the backs of my legs were painful for the next few
days!

All too soon, it was time for me to leave Baguio and return
to Bacnotan, but I had been greatly refreshed, and felt ready
for my next stint of teaching. Theresa accompanied me,
travelling first on the bus, and then on a tricycle. It had been

arranged for us to be picked up at Benguet, but on our arrival, no one was there.

We were approached by several men and all too soon I realised the potential dangers of two women travelling alone at night. We stood in the street and cried out to God to help us. Almost immediately a bike with a sidecar arrived and we recognised it as the one from the Bible College. Thank you Jesus, perfect timing! I shall never forget the journey home, every bump in the road felt wonderful. I looked up at the heavens on a crystal clear night; I never knew that there were so many stars. What a lovely welcome at CBI with the students rushing round to greet me. You would think that I had been away for months. There was a lovely meal waiting for me, and all my washing had been laundered. *Maday dayau ti Apo!* (Praise the Lord!)

Theresa left the following day to return to Baguio, but arranged that she would come and fetch me in two weeks time and take me back there once again. It was sad to see her go, and I shall always be grateful of her care and support to me.

There seemed to be much work to be done before the end of term and the examinations. The students were very attentive and encouraging and I loved being with them and getting to know them. We learnt together, shared together and laughed together. When the time came for their examinations, I was so pleased with their efforts. It had made everything worthwhile. Freddy, one of male students stood up and said how blessed he had been to have been taught by an English teacher, an opportunity that he would never have thought possible. It was a very moving moment for me. If anyone had told me a few years ago that I would be working in the Philippines, I too would have thought that unbelievable!

One day, after lessons, Sister Rebecca handed me sixteen letters from home. I went up to the veranda area, to seek solace and to eagerly read my mail. What a time to reflect upon the goodness of our Lord. There is something beautiful about this place in the evenings. When evening comes, it takes on a special beauty of its own, as the sun turns red and everything reflects a golden pink. I watched the farmers beginning to wend their way home with their caribaou, after a hard day's work. I could still see the women and children working in the fields, hear the goats bleating and watch the chickens forever scratching to find that tasty morsel. The rice fields are rotated yearly, and after last year's crop, the fields were being prepared to grow tobacco. Apparently the sight is spectacular in March, but the smell is not so appealing when the leaves are being prepared. As I drank in the view, it reminded me of a Constable painting. But all too soon it is over as darkness falls and out come the mosquitoes with vengeance. Urrh!

There were times when I could have allowed loneliness to be my companion, but the Holy Spirit continually reminded me of the Word:

'Draw near to God, and He will draw near to you.'
(James 4:8)

My relationship grew with the Lord in these moments and I really felt as if I was on honeymoon with Him again. I remembered the time when I was a little girl and wanting to be a disciple, not knowing then of course that you could be. The Lord told me that He had chosen me to serve Him in exactly that way. I indeed have found contentment, fulfilment and pure joy in doing just that. Let the Lord have His way in your life also, you will never regret it for one moment.

Chapter 18

Sad Goodbyes
and Homeward Bound

'Go into all the world and preach the gospel to every creature.'
(Mark 16:15)

The term was drawing to an end, and we began to make preparations for Christmas. I returned to spend another weekend with Theresa and her family. I was beginning to feel very tired and needed the rest. My ear problem was still causing me pain; so on my return to San Fernando Tracy Newlove took me to see a doctor. He put me on a course of antibiotics, after explaining that I had a severe middle ear infection and that I would not be able to fly home unless it had cleared up. In spite of the circumstances, I knew that the Lord would get me on that 'plane.

I returned to the Bible College and another warm welcome, especially from Cathy who ran into my arms. Whilst resting in my room, nursing her, I asked the Lord to speak to me. I heard the gentle inner voice of the Holy Spirit say, 'Make the most of every day at CBI.'

I realised that I only had just over a week left before I would begin my journey home. In some ways, that week was to prove to be the most difficult.

A wedding was to be held at the college, and a pig was duly brought and tethered to a tree. He lay in the hot sun for two days, as the preparations got under way. The wood was gradually collected and placed in a pile ... I wondered whether the pig knew what it was for! When his time was up I buried my head in my pillow to muffle the sound of his squealing as he was being slaughtered. The next time I saw him he was in little pieces in a big pot. The wedding and celebration went on for most of the day, and true to tradition, the bride was beautiful.

The final day arrived. I had mixed feelings as I packed my bags and prepared to say my goodbyes. Physically, I was ready to return home. Emotionally, I was torn, knowing the joy of seeing my family once again, but leaving my Filipino friends behind would not be easy. The Lord had shown me much and had given me much to think about on my journey home. Andy came to pick me up to take me to their house where I would spend the night. The next day we would all go to Manila together. I said my goodbyes to everyone at CBI and we shed a few tears together. I spent that night resting at Andy and Tracy's home as we had an early morning start ahead of us.

Andy and Tracy had a large selection of books and I picked up one entitled *Heartcry for China* by Ross Patterson. As I began to turn the pages, Tracy called me out of my room because she wanted me to meet a Chinese couple that had just come to live and work alongside the Chinese Church in San Fernando. Looking back, as I recall these incidents, I can see that God was beginning to speak to me and prepare me for His future calling on my life.

We left the following morning at 4.30 a.m. to begin the eight-hour journey to Manila. We prayed and asked the Lord to protect us on our journey. Andy explained the importance of praying for protection every day and not just to assume that we would have it without asking. (Mary and Joseph assumed that Jesus was with their relatives when they 'lost' Him on their journey from Jerusalem; Luke 2:41–50.)

I was grateful for a comfortable seat in the back of their jeep and appreciated the air-conditioning even in the early hours of the morning. Tracy sat in the front as Andy drove. It was not long before both Tracy and I fell asleep. We had been travelling for about one-and-a-half hours, when I suddenly woke up. I noticed that Tracy had woken as well. I looked out of the window, and to my horror, I saw a large coach travelling on the wrong side of the road, immediately in front of us. I knew in that instant, that death was staring us in the face. At exactly the same time, all three of us shouted out '**Jesus!**' We only had a split second, and only had time to cry out the name of the Lord for deliverance. Angels must have come immediately to our aid, for the speeding coach was 'lifted' around our jeep and we escaped. I know that without the divine intervention I would not be here writing this book. It was an experience I will remember the rest of my life.

We drove into a McDonalds. (Yes! They can be found even in the Philippines.) It was the best breakfast I had eaten for a long time! We continued on our journey over bumpy roads and onto dusty tracks that took us through the main devastation that had been caused two years previously from the eruption of Mount Pinatubo. It was, like driving on the moon's surface. Thick grey dust lay everywhere, preventing vegetation from growing. Whole villages lay many feet below its surface. As we travelled over this remote barren area I noticed, in the distance, a small boy standing at the side of the road. He was wrapped in a long cloak that covered his face and head. He was obviously just waiting for any passing vehicle and an opportunity to beg. I wanted to give this young boy money, and so I asked Andy if he would stop our jeep. As we slowed down, the young boy jumped onto the side of the vehicle and pushing his hand through the opened window, I placed some money into his small brown palm. As we drove off I watched him running towards his mother and small brothers and sisters, shouting excitedly and clutching his morning's work. It could be many hours before another opportunity would come their way.

Several hours later, we reached the safe haven of 'Shalom Bata Rescue Centre'. It was lovely to see all the children again and to meet the new arrivals. I was sad that Marchella was not there, but very happy to learn that she had been re-united with her father. Eventually the day arrived for my homeward bound journey. One of the Filipino workers who came to say goodbye accepted Jesus as her Lord and Saviour. It was a wonderful way to leave the Philippines. I was so happy as I left for the airport to board the flight to England.

After a brief stopover at Bangkok airport, I boarded the flight to Amsterdam. After the evening meal, the cabin crew settled the passengers for the night flight ahead. I do not find it easy to sleep on airplanes, but I must have 'dozed off' because I suddenly woke up. The 'plane was in darkness and I could just see that the other passengers sleeping. There was no sign of any activity. I have been told that the flight deck crew often doze themselves once the aircraft has been switched to autopilot. I do not know how true this is but it was a strange experience to think that perhaps I was the only person awake. I had a desire to worship the Lord and began to sing softly the lovely words of the chorus:

Father, I love You, I worship and adore You,
Glorify Your Name in all the earth,
Glorify Your Name, Glorify Your Name,
Glorify Your Name in all the earth.

Jesus I love You, I worship and adore You,
Glorify Your Name in all the earth,
Glorify Your Name, Glorify Your Name,
Glorify Your Name in all the earth.

I reached to open the window blind by my seat and looked out. The earth below me was also in darkness, with the exception of tiny clusters of lights. These lights picked out the cities below as we flew over the vast country of Russia. The Holy Spirit brought to my mind John 3:16:

> *'For God so loved the world that He gave His only begotten Son, that whoever believes in Him should not perish but have everlasting life.'*

The soft voice of the Holy Spirit reminded me that we Christians are the lights of the world. A world full of people living in spiritual darkness, a world full of people dying daily and going to a lost eternity; people who have never heard of Jesus Christ. In that moment I felt the burden and grief of our Father.

> **He has done everything that He could have done for the human race.**
> **He sent His Son for us.**

Jesus has done everything possible for us, paying the price for our sinful nature and dying for us individually.

We have been given the Holy Spirit to teach and guide us, to give us the power and authority to use the name of Jesus. We have the Spirit of God dwelling inside us. We have been equipped to

> *'Go into all the world and preach the gospel to every creature.'*
> (Mark 16:15)

Let us all fulfil that calling with urgency in our hearts.

Epilogue

I did not return to the Philippines as I had expected. God closed the door. But He was doing another work in my life and gently preparing me for a different direction. I spent many months feeling frustrated and uncertain, but God showed me that waiting is a very important part of preparation. I wrote down everything I felt He was saying to me and pondered them in my heart. Meanwhile, I had the privilege to travel to Spain and Israel to share and meet with others. Finally, through His word, several dreams and a prophecy, I knew that I was being called to serve the Lord in China.

In the early spring of 1997, I visited Hong Kong, and working with other Christians, carried Bibles into Mainland China. I have subsequently made several more trips and am now in the process of trying to learn to speak Mandarin. I believe my calling is to help the orphaned children and abandoned babies and to minister God's love to the many Chinese people.

'Now a woman . . . who had spent all her livelihood on physicians and could not be healed by any, came from behind and touched the border of His garment . . . And Jesus said, "Who touched Me?"'
(Luke 8:43–45)

Thank you for reading this book. If you are not a Christian, I hope you know how much God loves you and wants to have a personal relationship with you. There may be many things you do not understand and many questions you want to ask. That is quite normal, but God encourages you to come to Him just as you are. He will show you as you seek Him. He is longing to set you free and give you eternal life.

If you are already a Christian, I hope that you have been challenged and blessed by what you have read. I hope the Lord has spoken to you personally. Perhaps He is calling you to go to the foreign mission field. The need is great and there has never been a better opportunity than now to take up that challenge.

You may like to pray a prayer similar to the one I prayed in the first chapter. Be assured that once you have, you belong to Him. Try and find other Christians who love Jesus and who will help and encourage you. It is important that you go to a church that moves in the Holy Spirit. Ask God and I am sure He will show you where He wants you to go.

Begin to read your Bible, perhaps starting with the gospel of John. Remember the Holy Spirit will teach and guide you. Talk to Him as if He was your close friend, because that is what He wants to be.

> 'This is a faithful saying and worthy of all acceptance, that Christ Jesus came into the world to save sinners, of whom I am chief.' (1 Timothy 1:15)

'Heavenly Father, I pray for everyone who has read this book. Father, I ask that you will save those that are lost, heal those that are sick and comfort those who mourn.

May the Holy Spirit minister to every reader now and I ask it in Jesus' name. Amen.'